ON THE ODD HOURS

A tale by Eric Liberge

A piece of art is exactly like a child.
Or like an orphan, rather. When you're there before it,
and are admiring it with all your heart,
a privileged contact is created between the two of you.
It becomes your mirror.

Remove that simple attention from it, and it becomes nothing.

MUSÉE DU
LOUVRE
ÉDITIONS

Musée du Louvre

Henri Loyrette
President and Director

Didier Selles
General Administrator

Catherine Sueur
Assistant General Administrator

Christophe Monin
Head of Cultural Development

Violaine Bouvet-Lanselle
Head of the Publishing Service, Office of Cultural Development

Publishing

Series Editor: Fabrice Douar
Publishing Service, Office of Cultural Development, Musée du Louvre

Dedicated to my brother Nicolas, who is deaf, as well as his wife and all
those who live in "the world of silence."
Eric Liberge

ISBN 978-1-56163-577-1
Library of Congress Control Number: 2009943903
© Futuropolis / Musee du Louvre Editions 2008
© 2010 NBM for the English translation
Translation by Joe Johnson
Lettering by Ortho
Printed in Hong Kong
3 2 1

ComicsLit is an imprint
and trademark of

NANTIER • BEALL • MINOUSTCHINE
Publishing inc.
new york

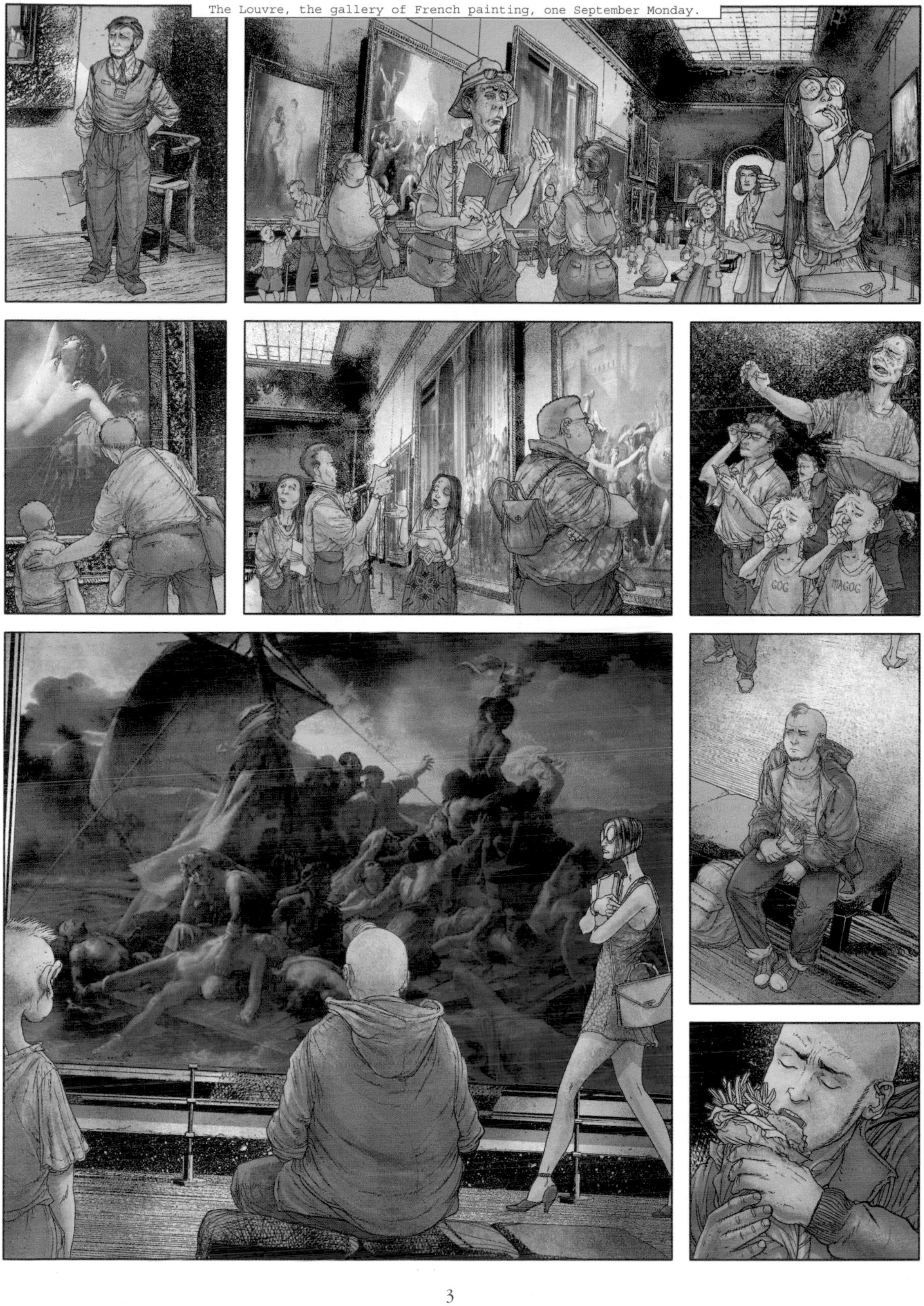
The Louvre, the gallery of French painting, one September Monday.
GOG
MAGOG

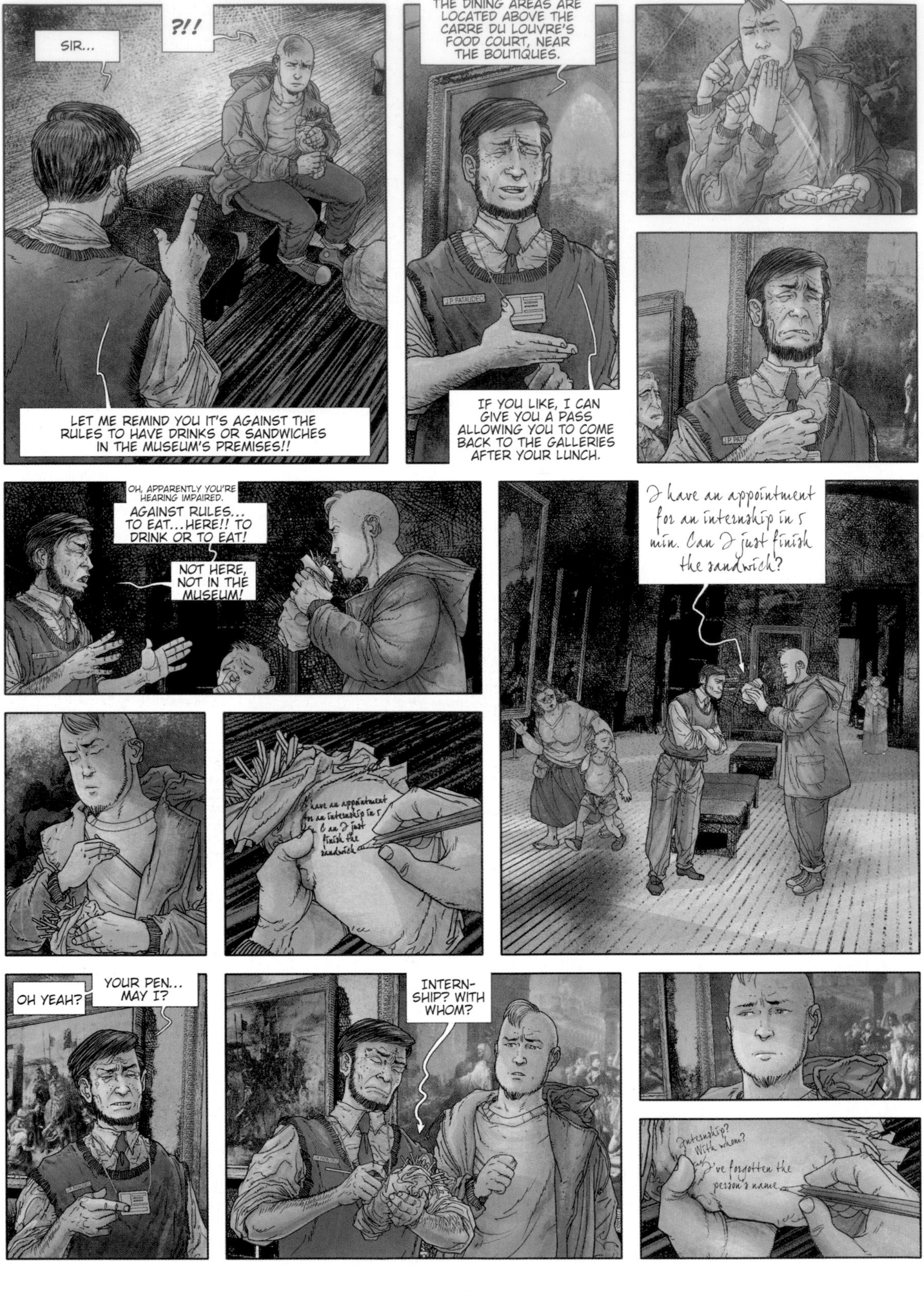
SIR...
?!!
LET ME REMIND YOU IT'S AGAINST THE RULES TO HAVE DRINKS OR SANDWICHES IN THE MUSEUM'S PREMISES!!
THE DINING AREAS ARE LOCATED ABOVE THE CARRE DU LOUVRE'S FOOD COURT, NEAR THE BOUTIQUES.
J.P. PATAUDEC
IF YOU LIKE, I CAN GIVE YOU A PASS ALLOWING YOU TO COME BACK TO THE GALLERIES AFTER YOUR LUNCH.
OH, APPARENTLY YOU'RE HEARING IMPAIRED.
AGAINST RULES... TO EAT...HERE!! TO DRINK OR TO EAT!
NOT HERE, NOT IN THE MUSEUM!
have an appointment
for an internship in 5
finish the
sandwich
I have an appointment for an internship in 5 min. Can I just finish the sandwich?
OH YEAH?
YOUR PEN... MAY I?
INTERN-SHIP? WITH WHOM?
Internship? With whom?
I've forgotten the person's name.

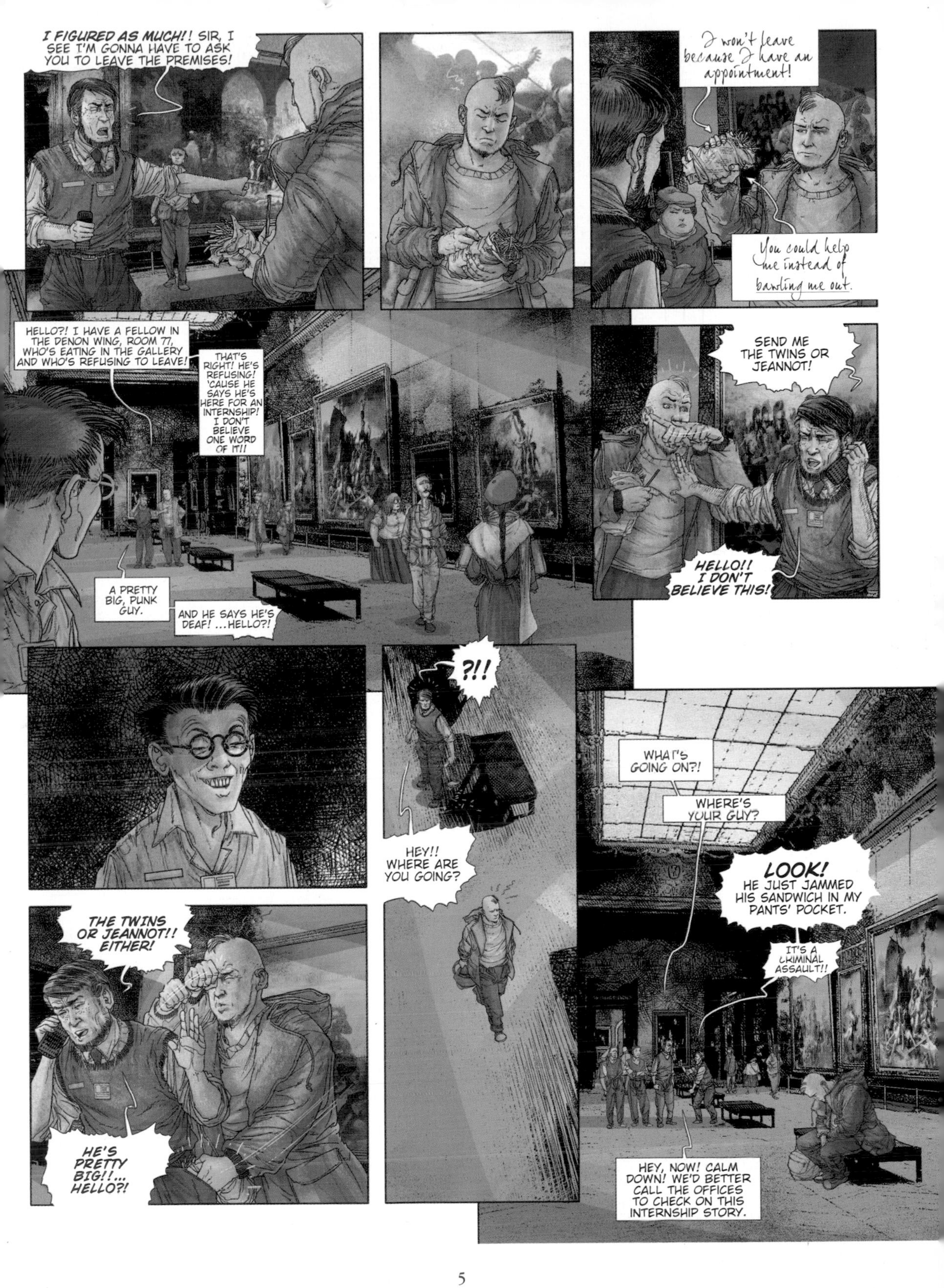
I FIGURED AS MUCH!! SIR, I SEE I'M GONNA HAVE TO ASK YOU TO LEAVE THE PREMISES!
I won't leave because I have an appointment!
You could help me instead of bawling me out.
HELLO?! I HAVE A FELLOW IN THE DENON WING, ROOM 77, WHO'S EATING IN THE GALLERY AND WHO'S REFUSING TO LEAVE!
THAT'S RIGHT! HE'S REFUSING! 'CAUSE HE SAYS HE'S HERE FOR AN INTERNSHIP! I DON'T BELIEVE ONE WORD OF IT!!
A PRETTY BIG, PUNK GUY.
AND HE SAYS HE'S DEAF! ...HELLO?!
SEND ME THE TWINS OR JEANNOT!
HELLO!! I DON'T BELIEVE THIS!
THE TWINS OR JEANNOT!! EITHER!
HE'S PRETTY BIG!!... HELLO?!
?!!
HEY!! WHERE ARE YOU GOING?
WHAT'S GOING ON?!
WHERE'S YOUR GUY?
LOOK! HE JUST JAMMED HIS SANDWICH IN MY PANTS' POCKET.
IT'S A CRIMINAL ASSAULT!!
HEY, NOW! CALM DOWN! WE'D BETTER CALL THE OFFICES TO CHECK ON THIS INTERNSHIP STORY.

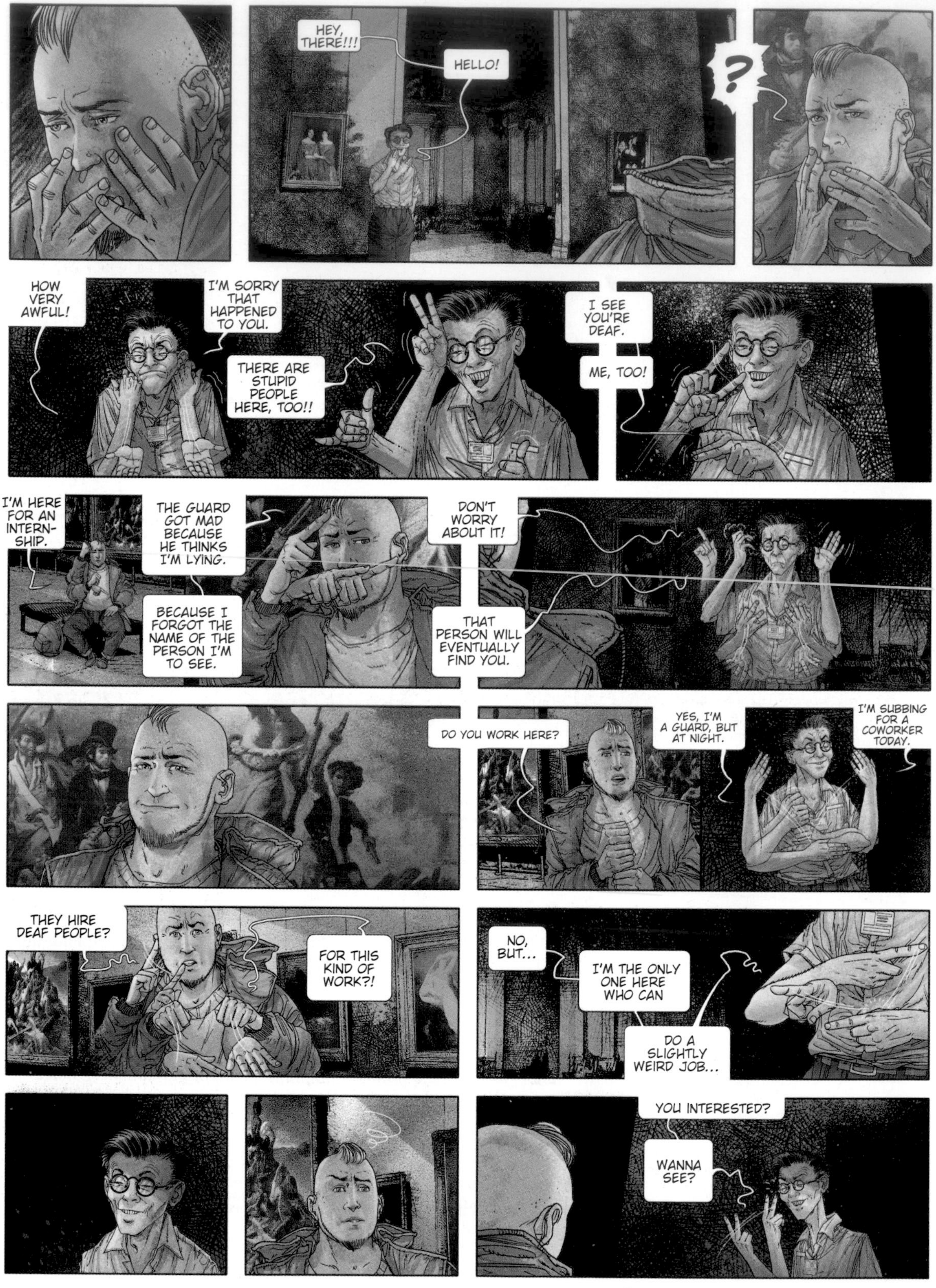
HEY, THERE!!!
HELLO!
?
HOW VERY AWFUL!
I'M SORRY THAT HAPPENED TO YOU.
THERE ARE STUPID PEOPLE HERE, TOO!!
I SEE YOU'RE DEAF.
ME, TOO!
I'M HERE FOR AN INTERN-SHIP.
THE GUARD GOT MAD BECAUSE HE THINKS I'M LYING.
BECAUSE I FORGOT THE NAME OF THE PERSON I'M TO SEE.
DON'T WORRY ABOUT IT!
THAT PERSON WILL EVENTUALLY FIND YOU.
DO YOU WORK HERE?
YES, I'M A GUARD, BUT AT NIGHT.
I'M SUBBING FOR A COWORKER TODAY.
THEY HIRE DEAF PEOPLE?
FOR THIS KIND OF WORK?!
NO, BUT...
I'M THE ONLY ONE HERE WHO CAN
DO A SLIGHTLY WEIRD JOB...
YOU INTERESTED?
WANNA SEE?

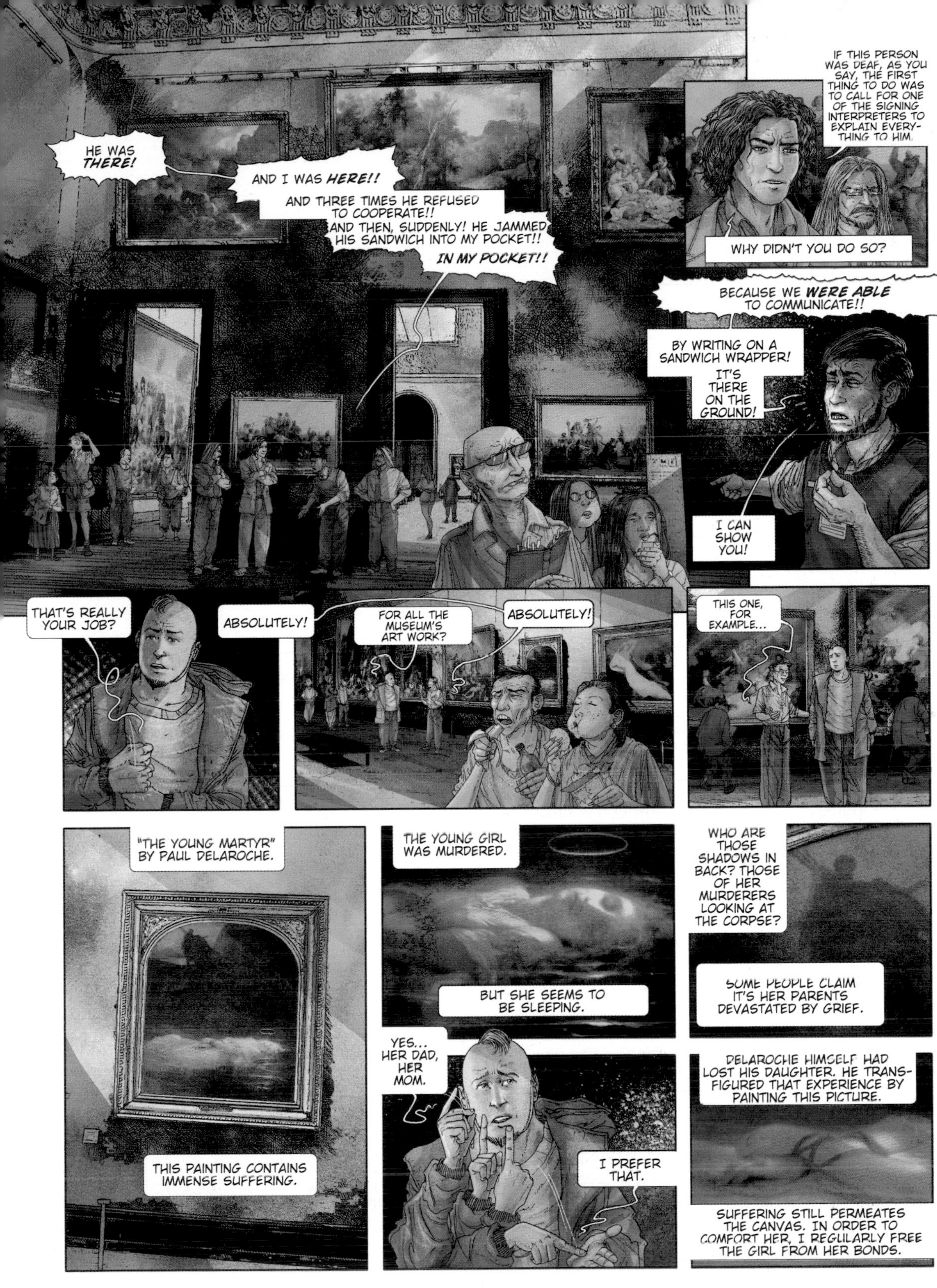

HE WAS THERE!
AND I WAS HERE!!
AND THREE TIMES HE REFUSED TO COOPERATE!!
AND THEN, SUDDENLY! HE JAMMED HIS SANDWICH INTO MY POCKET!!
IN MY POCKET!!
IF THIS PERSON WAS DEAF, AS YOU SAY, THE FIRST THING TO DO WAS TO CALL FOR ONE OF THE SIGNING INTERPRETERS TO EXPLAIN EVERYTHING TO HIM.
WHY DIDN'T YOU DO SO?
BECAUSE WE WERE ABLE TO COMMUNICATE!!
BY WRITING ON A SANDWICH WRAPPER!
IT'S THERE ON THE GROUND!
I CAN SHOW YOU!
THAT'S REALLY YOUR JOB?
ABSOLUTELY!
FOR ALL THE MUSEUM'S ART WORK?
ABSOLUTELY!
THIS ONE, FOR EXAMPLE...
"THE YOUNG MARTYR" BY PAUL DELAROCHE.
THIS PAINTING CONTAINS IMMENSE SUFFERING.
THE YOUNG GIRL WAS MURDERED.
BUT SHE SEEMS TO BE SLEEPING.
WHO ARE THOSE SHADOWS IN BACK? THOSE OF HER MURDERERS LOOKING AT THE CORPSE?
SOME PEOPLE CLAIM IT'S HER PARENTS DEVASTATED BY GRIEF.
YES... HER DAD, HER MOM.
I PREFER THAT.
DELAROCHE HIMSELF HAD LOST HIS DAUGHTER. HE TRANSFIGURED THAT EXPERIENCE BY PAINTING THIS PICTURE.
SUFFERING STILL PERMEATES THE CANVAS. IN ORDER TO COMFORT HER, I REGULARLY FREE THE GIRL FROM HER BONDS.

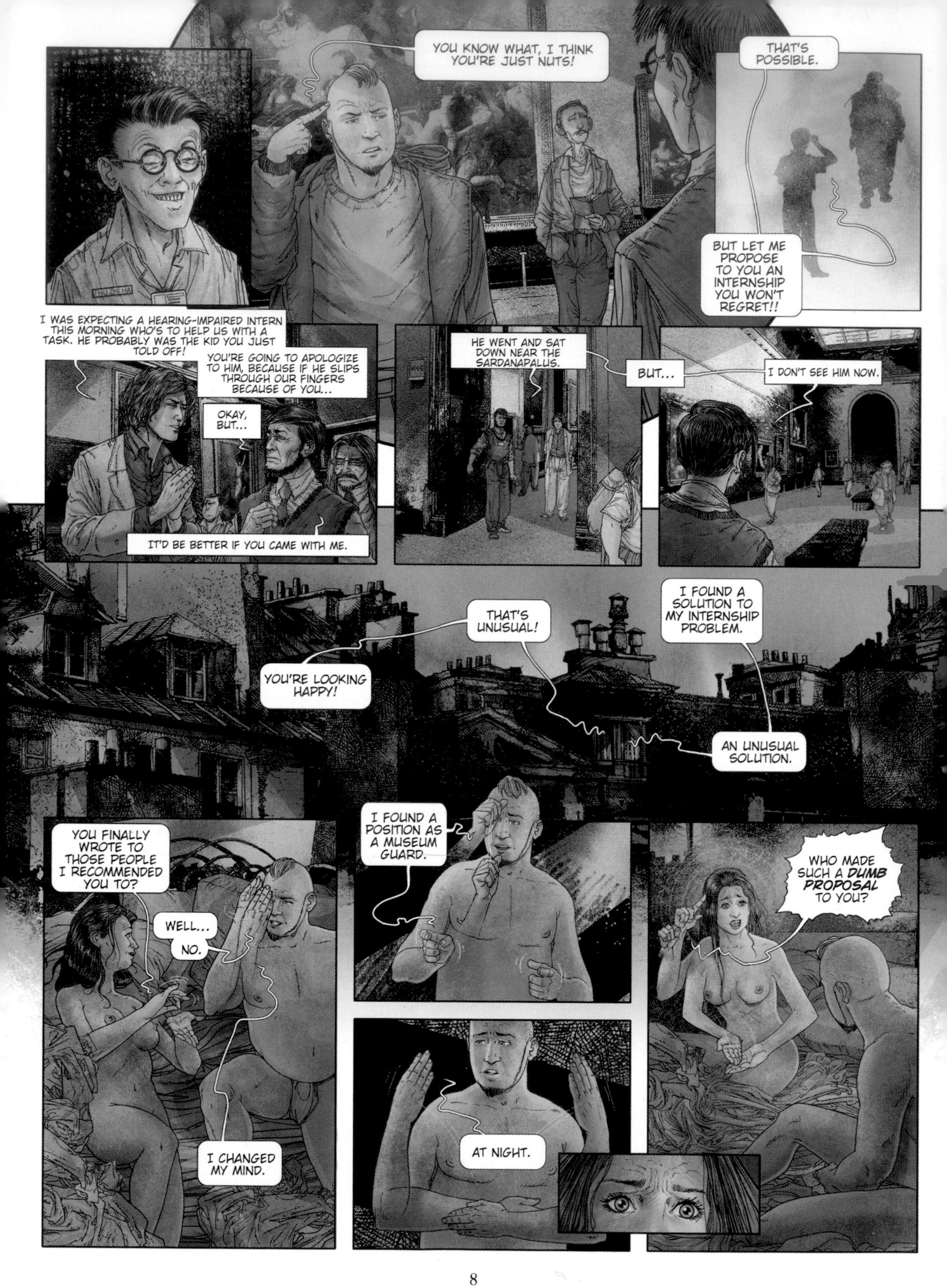
FHU ZHI HA
YOU KNOW WHAT, I THINK YOU'RE JUST NUTS!
THAT'S POSSIBLE.
BUT LET ME PROPOSE TO YOU AN INTERNSHIP YOU WON'T REGRET!!
I WAS EXPECTING A HEARING-IMPAIRED INTERN THIS MORNING WHO'S TO HELP US WITH A TASK. HE PROBABLY WAS THE KID YOU JUST TOLD OFF!
YOU'RE GOING TO APOLOGIZE TO HIM, BECAUSE IF HE SLIPS THROUGH OUR FINGERS BECAUSE OF YOU...
OKAY, BUT...
IT'D BE BETTER IF YOU CAME WITH ME.
HE WENT AND SAT DOWN NEAR THE SARDANAPALUS.
BUT...
I DON'T SEE HIM NOW.
YOU'RE LOOKING HAPPY!
THAT'S UNUSUAL!
I FOUND A SOLUTION TO MY INTERNSHIP PROBLEM.
AN UNUSUAL SOLUTION.
YOU FINALLY WROTE TO THOSE PEOPLE I RECOMMENDED YOU TO?
WELL...
NO.
I CHANGED MY MIND.
I FOUND A POSITION AS A MUSEUM GUARD.
AT NIGHT.
WHO MADE SUCH A DUMB PROPOSAL TO YOU?

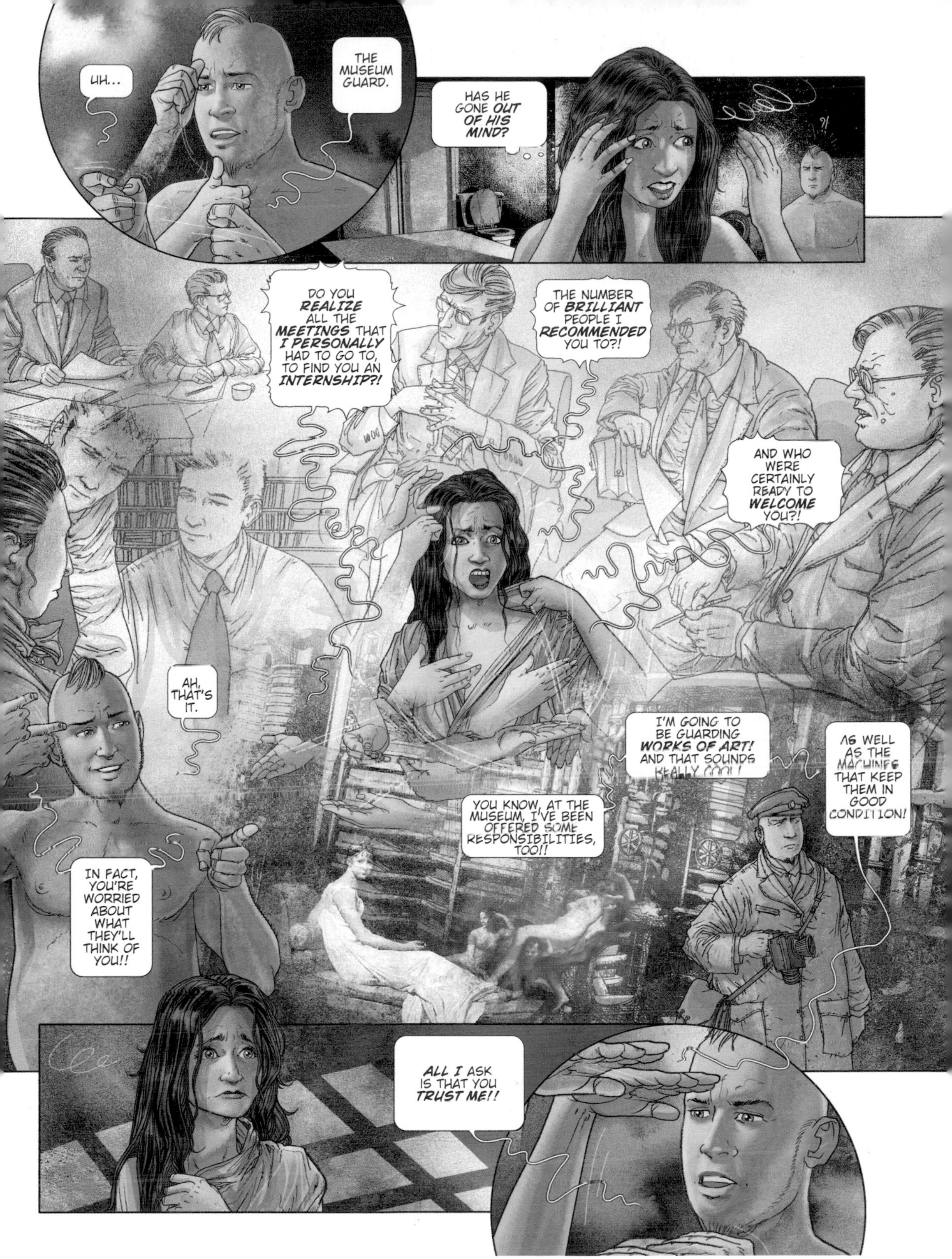
UH...
THE MUSEUM GUARD.
HAS HE GONE OUT OF HIS MIND?
?!
DO YOU REALIZE ALL THE MEETINGS THAT I PERSONALLY HAD TO GO TO, TO FIND YOU AN INTERNSHIP?!
THE NUMBER OF BRILLIANT PEOPLE I RECOMMENDED YOU TO?!
AND WHO WERE CERTAINLY READY TO WELCOME YOU?!
AH, THAT'S IT.
I'M GOING TO BE GUARDING WORKS OF ART! AND THAT SOUNDS REALLY COOL!
AS WELL AS THE MACHINES THAT KEEP THEM IN GOOD CONDITION!
YOU KNOW, AT THE MUSEUM, I'VE BEEN OFFERED SOME RESPONSIBILITIES, TOO!!
IN FACT, YOU'RE WORRIED ABOUT WHAT THEY'LL THINK OF YOU!!
ALL I ASK IS THAT YOU TRUST ME!!

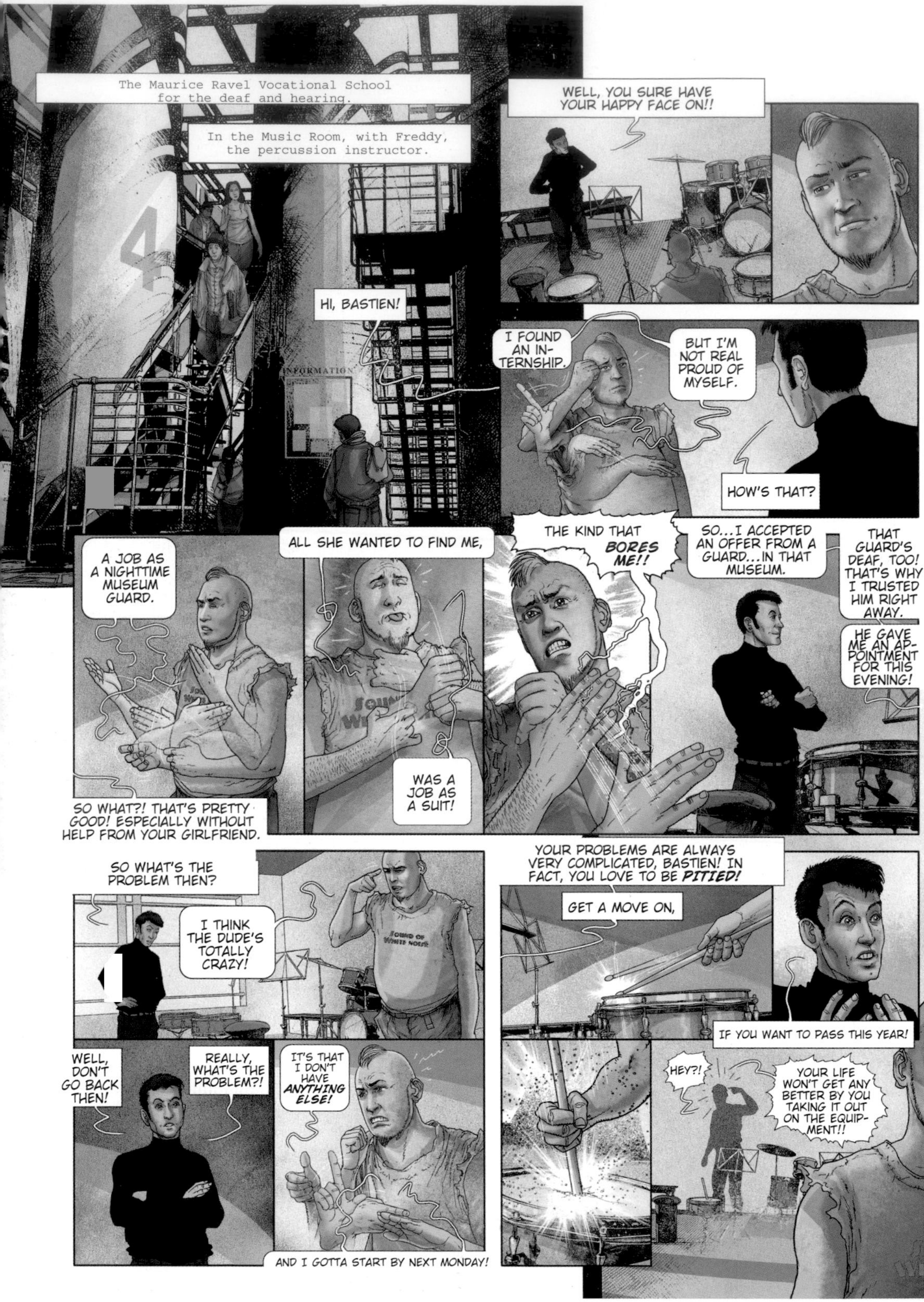

The Maurice Ravel Vocational School for the deaf and hearing.
In the Music Room, with Freddy, the percussion instructor.
HI, BASTIEN!
WELL, YOU SURE HAVE YOUR HAPPY FACE ON!!
I FOUND AN IN-TERNSHIP.
BUT I'M NOT REAL PROUD OF MYSELF.
HOW'S THAT?
A JOB AS A NIGHTTIME MUSEUM GUARD.
SO WHAT?! THAT'S PRETTY GOOD! ESPECIALLY WITHOUT HELP FROM YOUR GIRLFRIEND.
ALL SHE WANTED TO FIND ME,
WAS A JOB AS A SUIT!
THE KIND THAT BORES ME!!
SO...I ACCEPTED AN OFFER FROM A GUARD...IN THAT MUSEUM.
THAT GUARD'S DEAF, TOO! THAT'S WHY I TRUSTED HIM RIGHT AWAY.
HE GAVE ME AN AP-POINTMENT FOR THIS EVENING!
SO WHAT'S THE PROBLEM THEN?
I THINK THE DUDE'S TOTALLY CRAZY!
WELL, DON'T GO BACK THEN!
REALLY, WHAT'S THE PROBLEM?!
IT'S THAT I DON'T HAVE ANYTHING ELSE!
AND I GOTTA START BY NEXT MONDAY!
YOUR PROBLEMS ARE ALWAYS VERY COMPLICATED, BASTIEN! IN FACT, YOU LOVE TO BE PITIED!
GET A MOVE ON,
IF YOU WANT TO PASS THIS YEAR!
HEY?!
YOUR LIFE WON'T GET ANY BETTER BY YOU TAKING IT OUT ON THE EQUIP-MENT!!

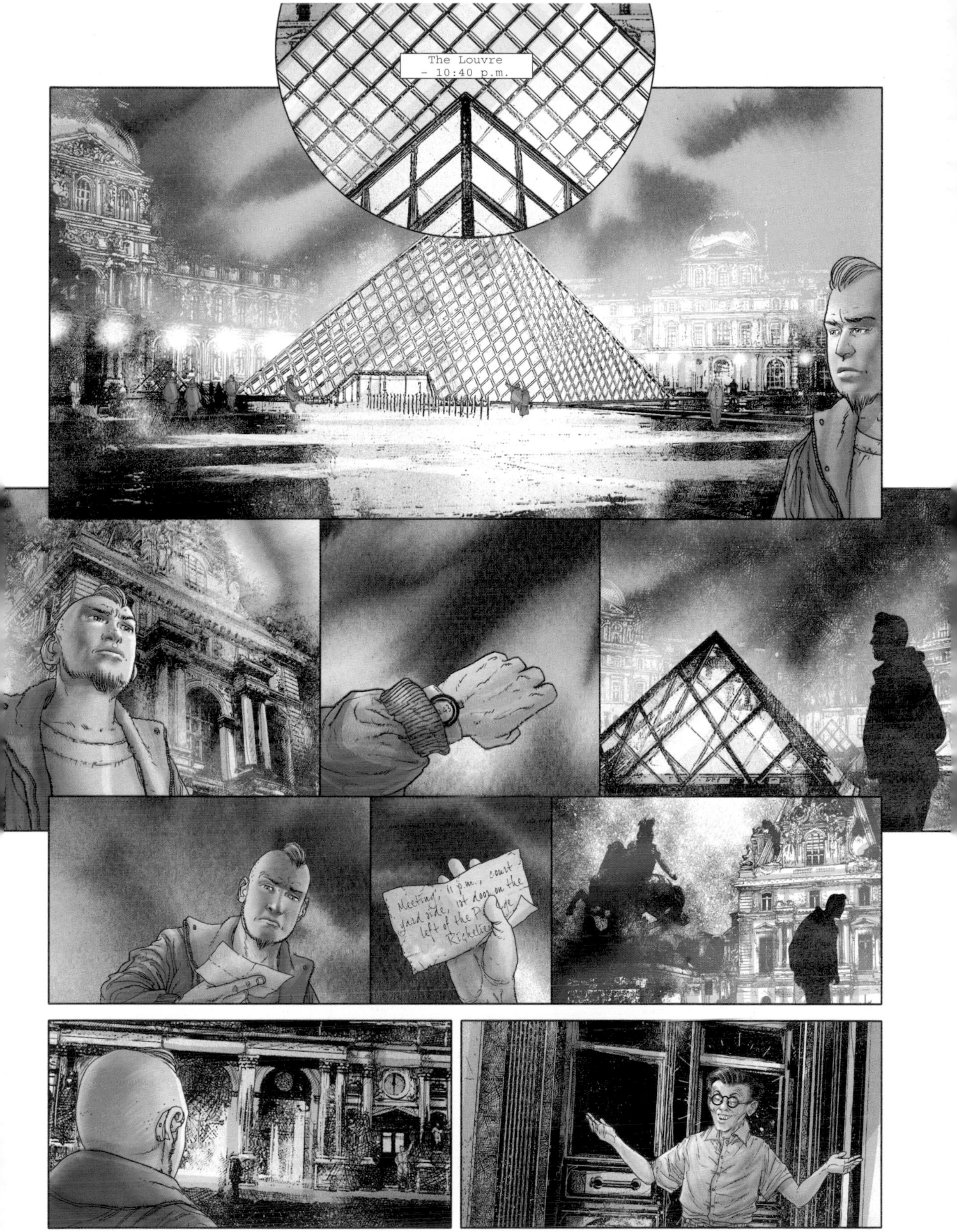
The Louvre
- 10:40 p.m.
Meeting, 11 p.m., court
yard side, 1st door on the
left of the

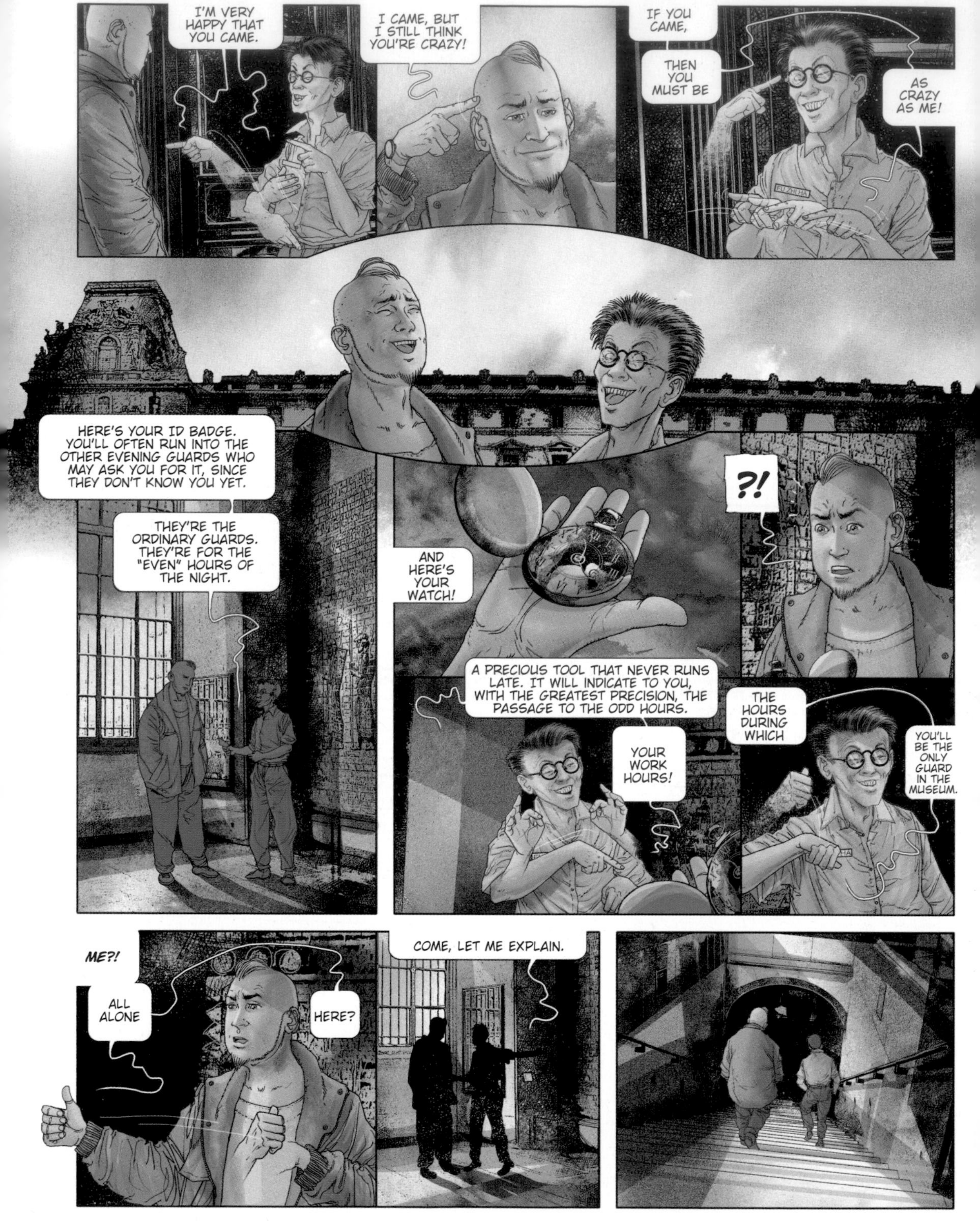
I'M VERY HAPPY THAT YOU CAME.
I CAME, BUT I STILL THINK YOU'RE CRAZY!
IF YOU CAME,
THEN YOU MUST BE
AS CRAZY AS ME!
HERE'S YOUR ID BADGE. YOU'LL OFTEN RUN INTO THE OTHER EVENING GUARDS WHO MAY ASK YOU FOR IT, SINCE THEY DON'T KNOW YOU YET.
THEY'RE THE ORDINARY GUARDS. THEY'RE FOR THE "EVEN" HOURS OF THE NIGHT.
AND HERE'S YOUR WATCH!
?!
A PRECIOUS TOOL THAT NEVER RUNS LATE. IT WILL INDICATE TO YOU, WITH THE GREATEST PRECISION, THE PASSAGE TO THE ODD HOURS.
YOUR WORK HOURS!
THE HOURS DURING WHICH
YOU'LL BE THE ONLY GUARD IN THE MUSEUM.
ME?!
ALL ALONE
HERE?
COME, LET ME EXPLAIN.

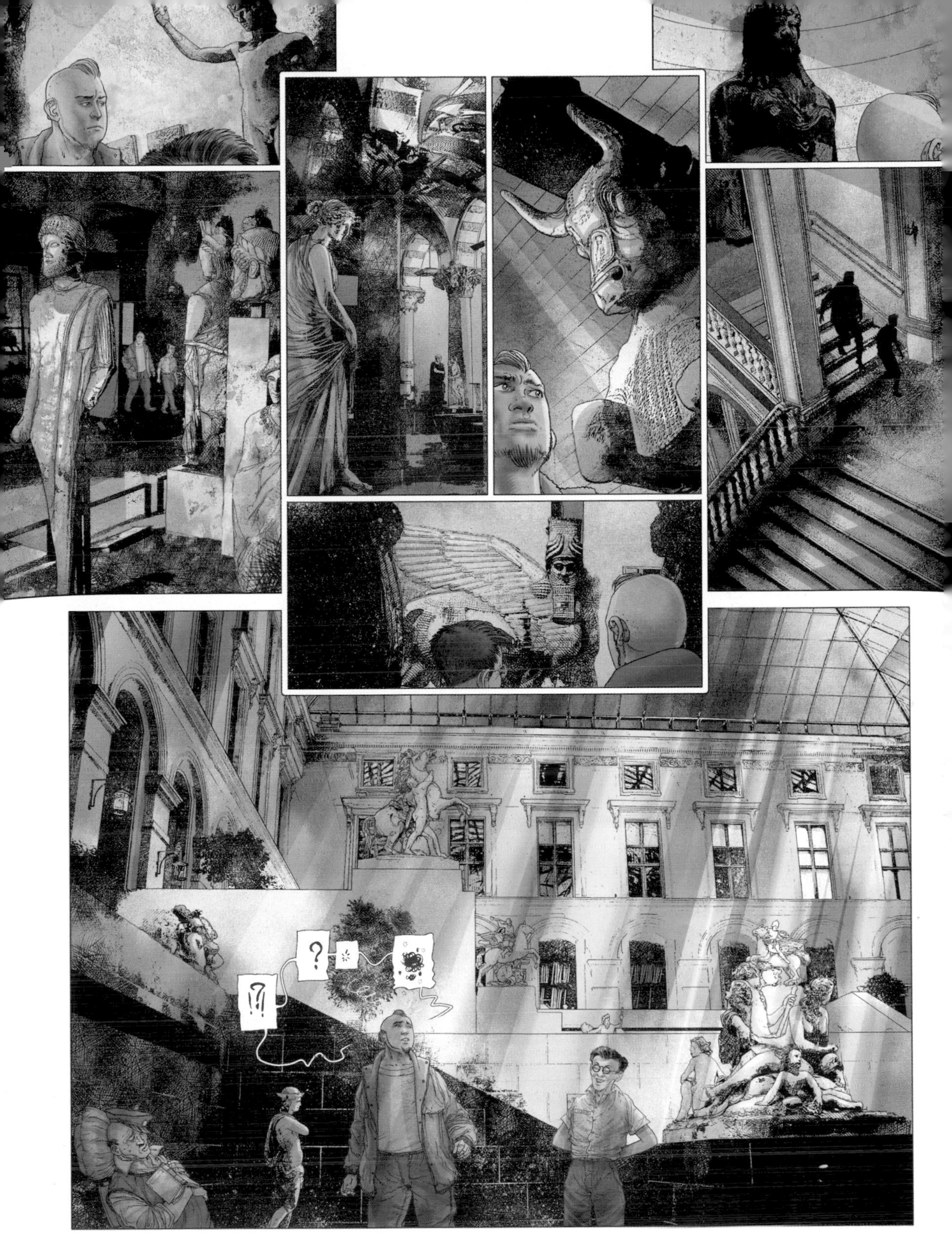
!?!
?

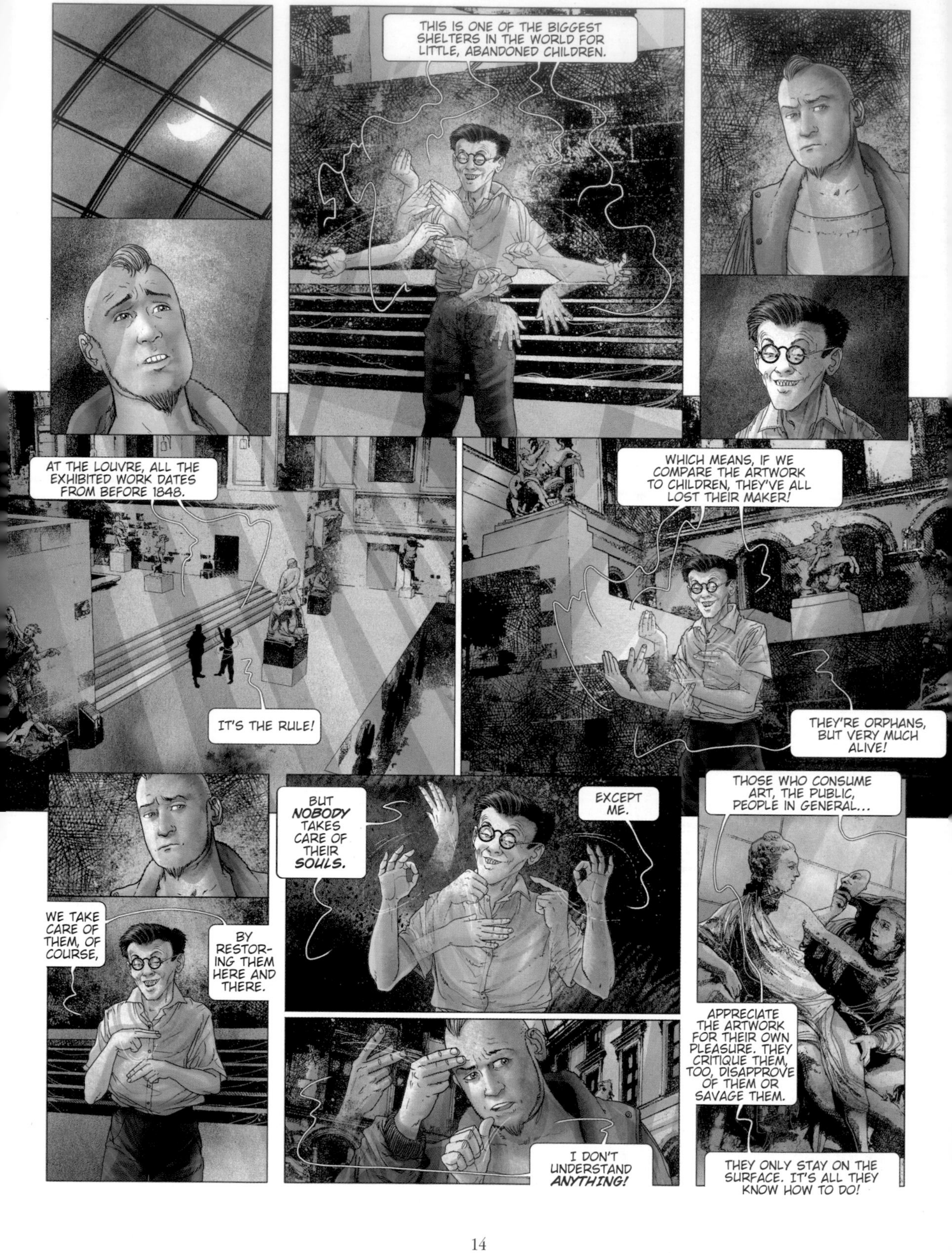
THIS IS ONE OF THE BIGGEST SHELTERS IN THE WORLD FOR LITTLE, ABANDONED CHILDREN.
AT THE LOUVRE, ALL THE EXHIBITED WORK DATES FROM BEFORE 1848.
IT'S THE RULE!
WHICH MEANS, IF WE COMPARE THE ARTWORK TO CHILDREN, THEY'VE ALL LOST THEIR MAKER!
THEY'RE ORPHANS, BUT VERY MUCH ALIVE!
WE TAKE CARE OF THEM, OF COURSE,
BY RESTOR-ING THEM HERE AND THERE.
BUT NOBODY TAKES CARE OF THEIR SOULS.
EXCEPT ME.
I DON'T UNDERSTAND ANYTHING!
THOSE WHO CONSUME ART, THE PUBLIC, PEOPLE IN GENERAL...
APPRECIATE THE ARTWORK FOR THEIR OWN PLEASURE. THEY CRITIQUE THEM, TOO, DISAPPROVE OF THEM OR SAVAGE THEM.
THEY ONLY STAY ON THE SURFACE. IT'S ALL THEY KNOW HOW TO DO!

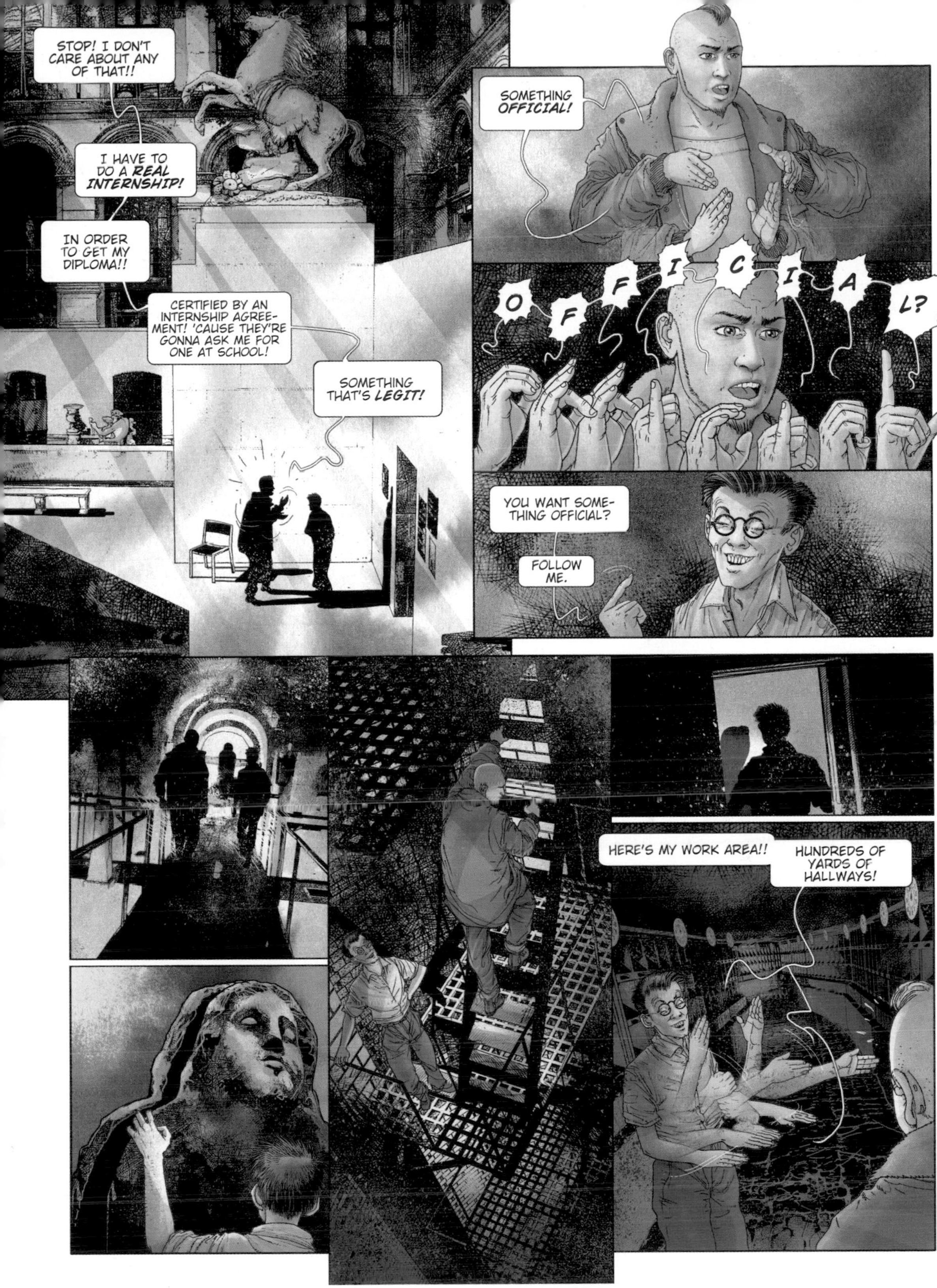
STOP! I DON'T CARE ABOUT ANY OF THAT!!
I HAVE TO DO A REAL INTERNSHIP!
IN ORDER TO GET MY DIPLOMA!!
CERTIFIED BY AN INTERNSHIP AGREEMENT! 'CAUSE THEY'RE GONNA ASK ME FOR ONE AT SCHOOL!
SOMETHING THAT'S LEGIT!
SOMETHING OFFICIAL!
O F F I C I A L?
YOU WANT SOMETHING OFFICIAL?
FOLLOW ME.
HERE'S MY WORK AREA!!
HUNDREDS OF YARDS OF HALLWAYS!

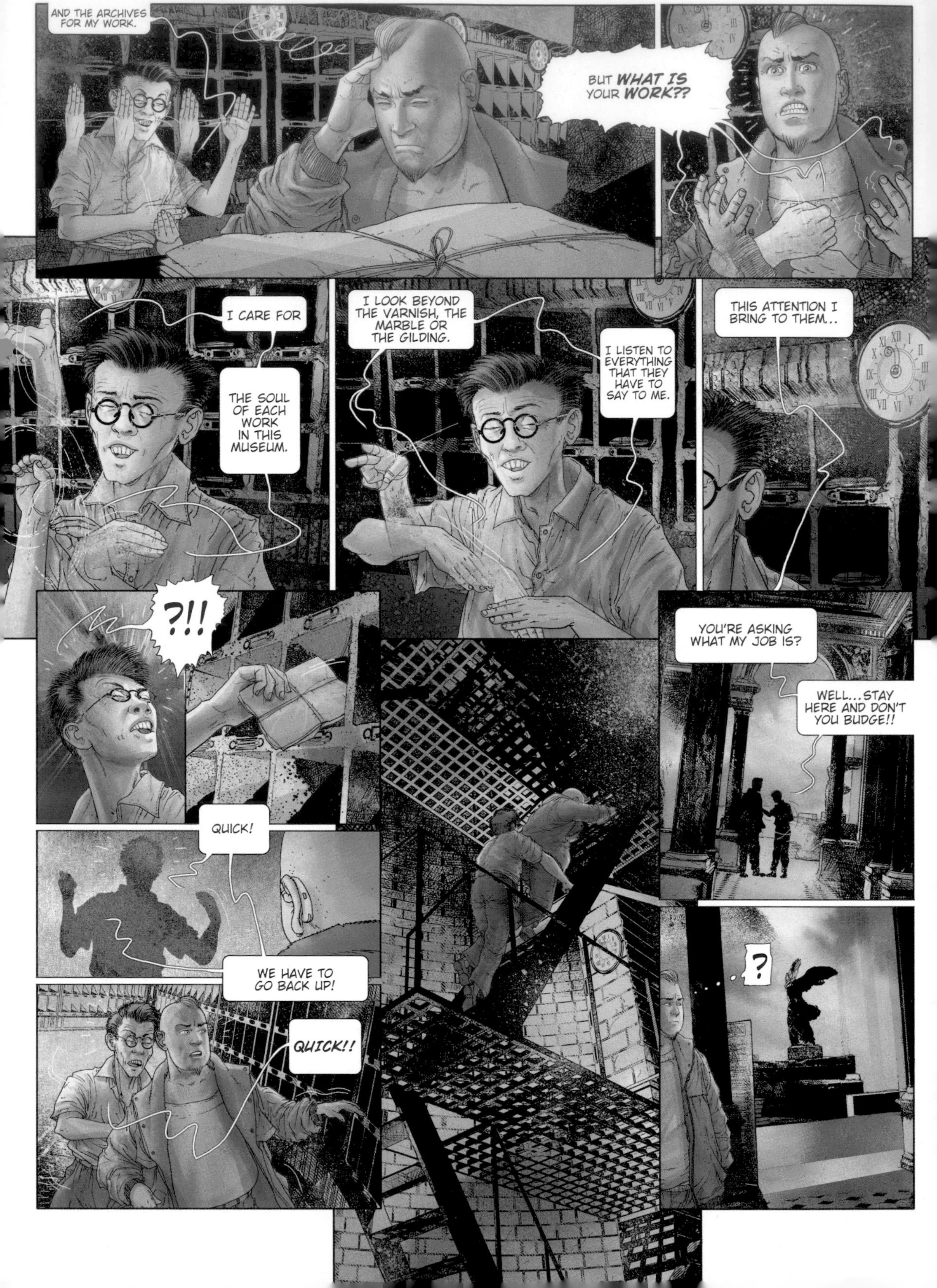
AND THE ARCHIVES FOR MY WORK.
BUT WHAT IS YOUR WORK??
I CARE FOR
THE SOUL OF EACH WORK IN THIS MUSEUM.
I LOOK BEYOND THE VARNISH, THE MARBLE OR THE GILDING.
I LISTEN TO EVERYTHING THAT THEY HAVE TO SAY TO ME.
THIS ATTENTION I BRING TO THEM...
?!!
QUICK!
WE HAVE TO GO BACK UP!
QUICK!!
YOU'RE ASKING WHAT MY JOB IS?
WELL... STAY HERE AND DON'T YOU BUDGE!!
?

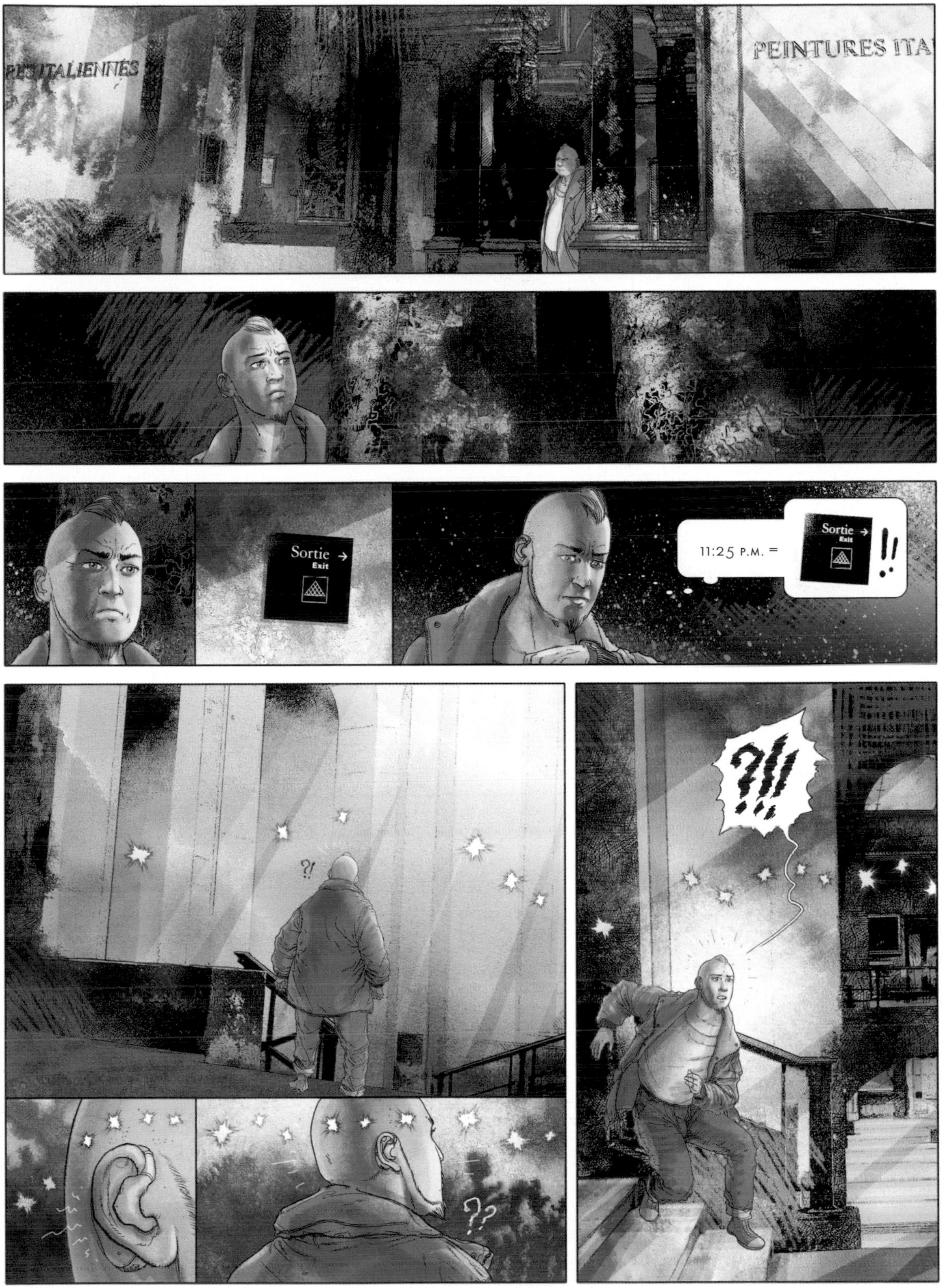

...ES ITALIENNES
PEINTURES ITA...
Sortie
Exit
11:25 P.M. =
Sortie
Exit
!!
?!
?!!
??

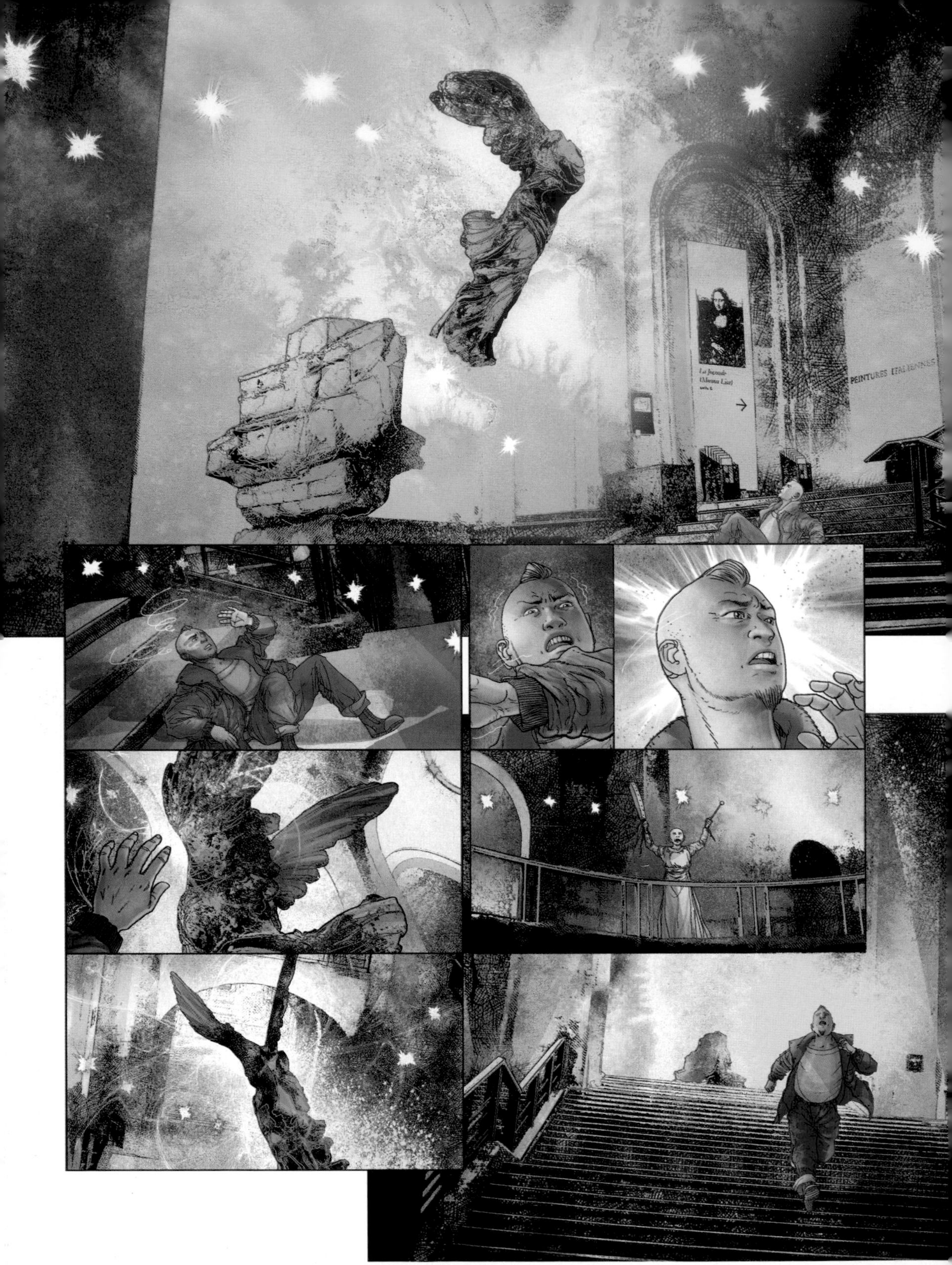
PEINTURES

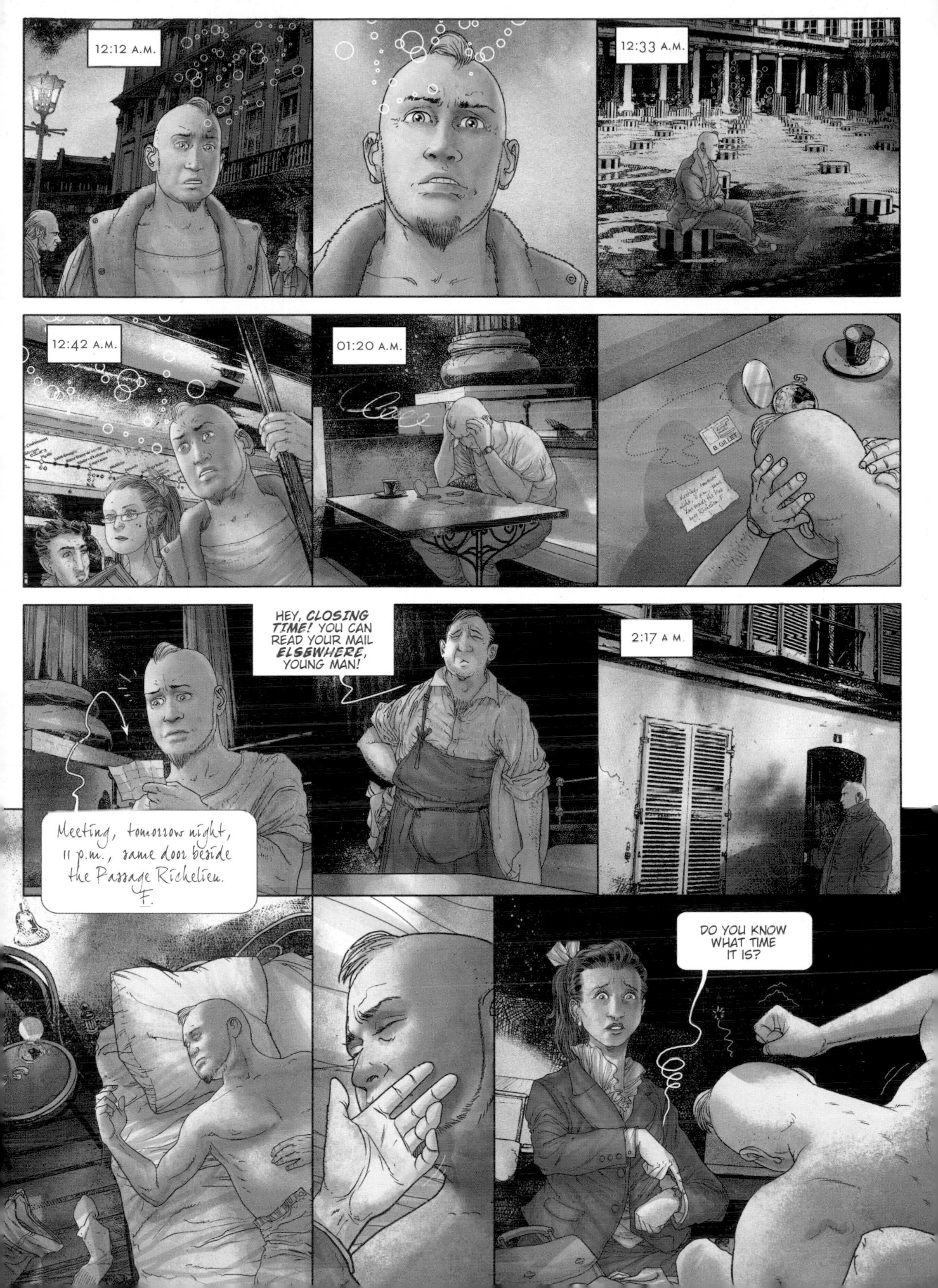
12:12 A.M.
12:33 A.M.
12:42 A.M.
01:20 A.M.
B. GILLET
HEY, CLOSING TIME! YOU CAN READ YOUR MAIL ELSEWHERE, YOUNG MAN!
2:17 A.M.
Meeting, tomorrow night, 11 p.m., same door beside the Passage Richelieu. F.
DO YOU KNOW WHAT TIME IT IS?

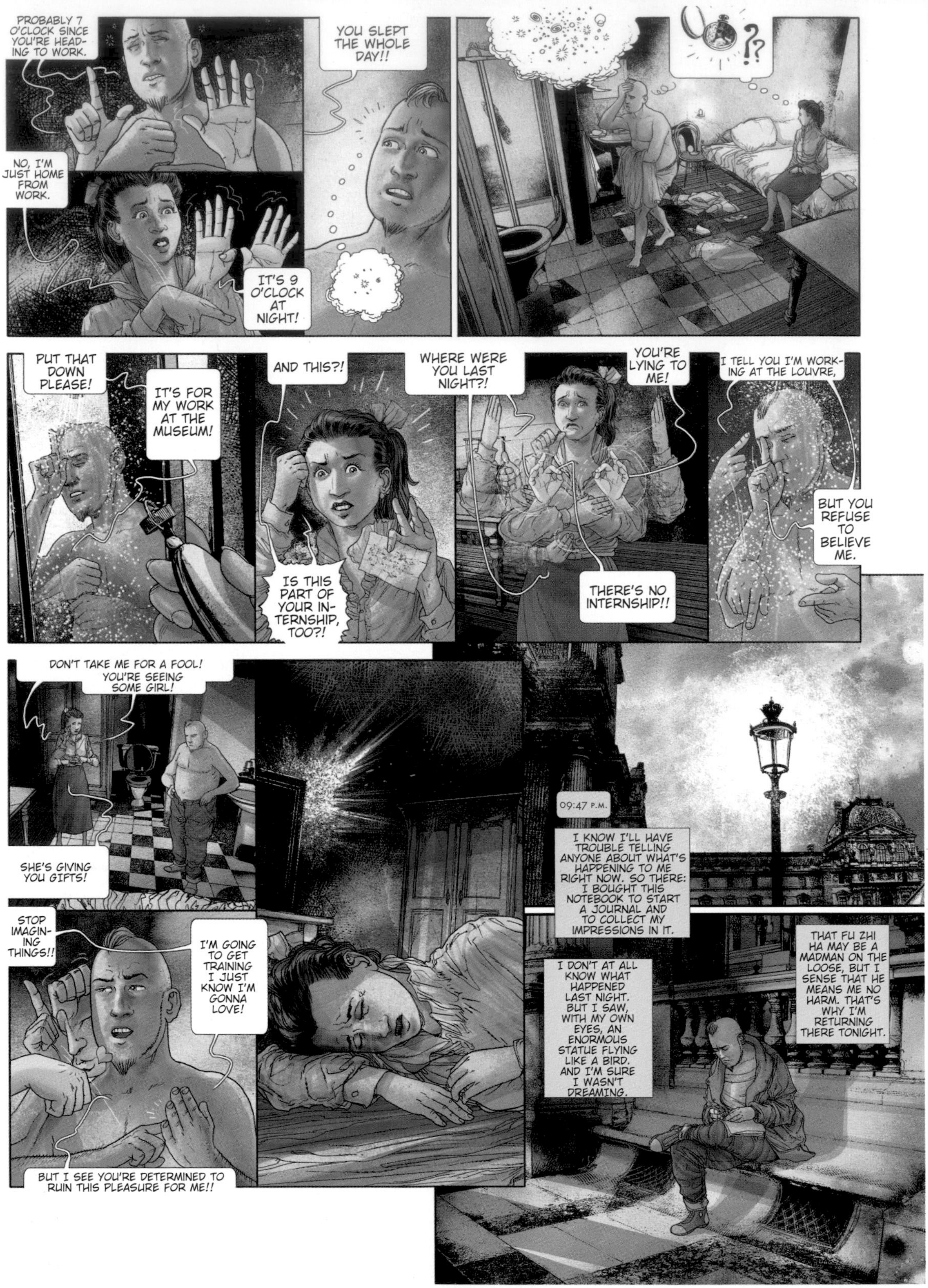
PROBABLY 7 O'CLOCK SINCE YOU'RE HEADING TO WORK.
NO, I'M JUST HOME FROM WORK.
YOU SLEPT THE WHOLE DAY!!
IT'S 9 O'CLOCK AT NIGHT!
PUT THAT DOWN PLEASE!
IT'S FOR MY WORK AT THE MUSEUM!
AND THIS?!
IS THIS PART OF YOUR INTERNSHIP, TOO?!
WHERE WERE YOU LAST NIGHT?!
YOU'RE LYING TO ME!
THERE'S NO INTERNSHIP!!
I TELL YOU I'M WORKING AT THE LOUVRE,
BUT YOU REFUSE TO BELIEVE ME.
DON'T TAKE ME FOR A FOOL! YOU'RE SEEING SOME GIRL!
SHE'S GIVING YOU GIFTS!
STOP IMAGINING THINGS!!
I'M GOING TO GET TRAINING I JUST KNOW I'M GONNA LOVE!
BUT I SEE YOU'RE DETERMINED TO RUIN THIS PLEASURE FOR ME!!
09:47 P.M.
I KNOW I'LL HAVE TROUBLE TELLING ANYONE ABOUT WHAT'S HAPPENING TO ME RIGHT NOW. SO THERE: I BOUGHT THIS NOTEBOOK TO START A JOURNAL AND TO COLLECT MY IMPRESSIONS IN IT.
I DON'T AT ALL KNOW WHAT HAPPENED LAST NIGHT. BUT I SAW, WITH MY OWN EYES, AN ENORMOUS STATUE FLYING LIKE A BIRD. AND I'M SURE I WASN'T DREAMING.
THAT FU ZHI HA MAY BE A MADMAN ON THE LOOSE, BUT I SENSE THAT HE MEANS ME NO HARM. THAT'S WHY I'M RETURNING THERE TONIGHT.

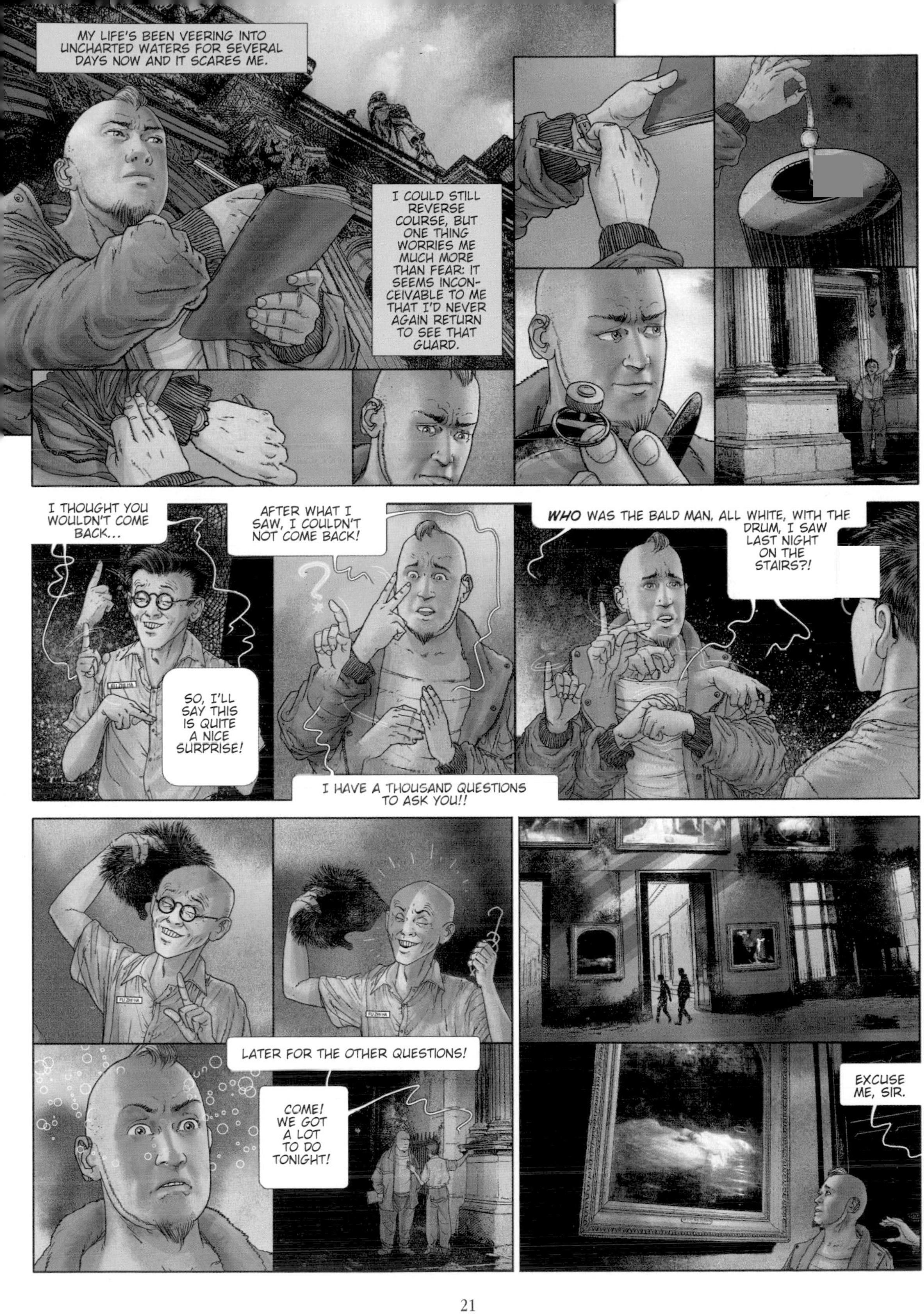

MY LIFE'S BEEN VEERING INTO UNCHARTED WATERS FOR SEVERAL DAYS NOW AND IT SCARES ME.
I COULD STILL REVERSE COURSE, BUT ONE THING WORRIES ME MUCH MORE THAN FEAR: IT SEEMS INCONCEIVABLE TO ME THAT I'D NEVER AGAIN RETURN TO SEE THAT GUARD.
I THOUGHT YOU WOULDN'T COME BACK...
SO, I'LL SAY THIS IS QUITE A NICE SURPRISE!
AFTER WHAT I SAW, I COULDN'T NOT COME BACK!
I HAVE A THOUSAND QUESTIONS TO ASK YOU!!
WHO WAS THE BALD MAN, ALL WHITE, WITH THE DRUM, I SAW LAST NIGHT ON THE STAIRS?!
LATER FOR THE OTHER QUESTIONS!
COME! WE GOT A LOT TO DO TONIGHT!
EXCUSE ME, SIR.

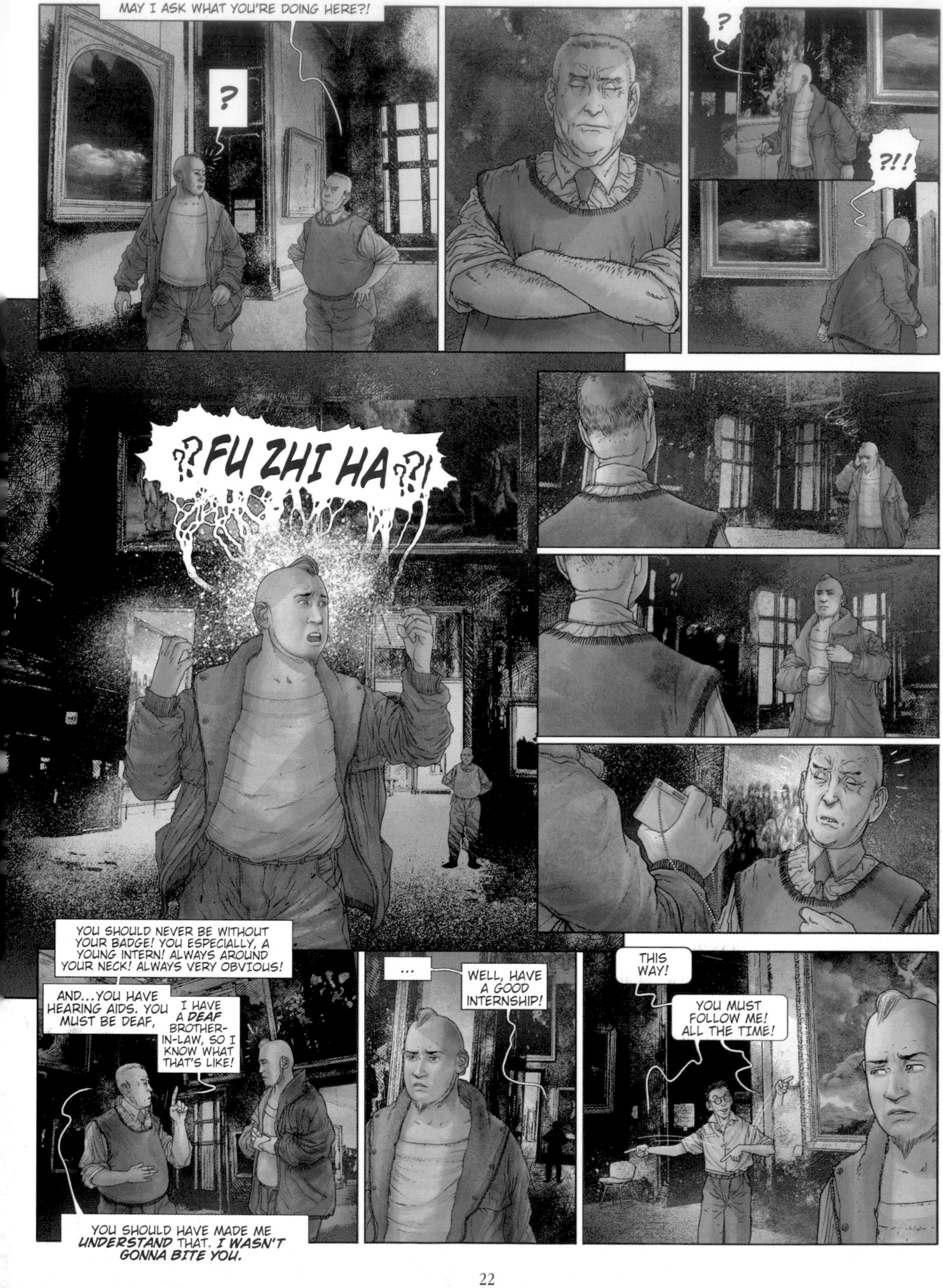
MAY I ASK WHAT YOU'RE DOING HERE?!
?
?
?!!
?FU ZHI HA?!
?!
YOU SHOULD NEVER BE WITHOUT YOUR BADGE! YOU ESPECIALLY, A YOUNG INTERN! ALWAYS AROUND YOUR NECK! ALWAYS VERY OBVIOUS!
AND...YOU HAVE HEARING AIDS. YOU MUST BE DEAF,
I HAVE A DEAF BROTHER-IN-LAW, SO I KNOW WHAT THAT'S LIKE!
YOU SHOULD HAVE MADE ME UNDERSTAND THAT. I WASN'T GONNA BITE YOU.
...
WELL, HAVE A GOOD INTERNSHIP!
THIS WAY!
YOU MUST FOLLOW ME! ALL THE TIME!

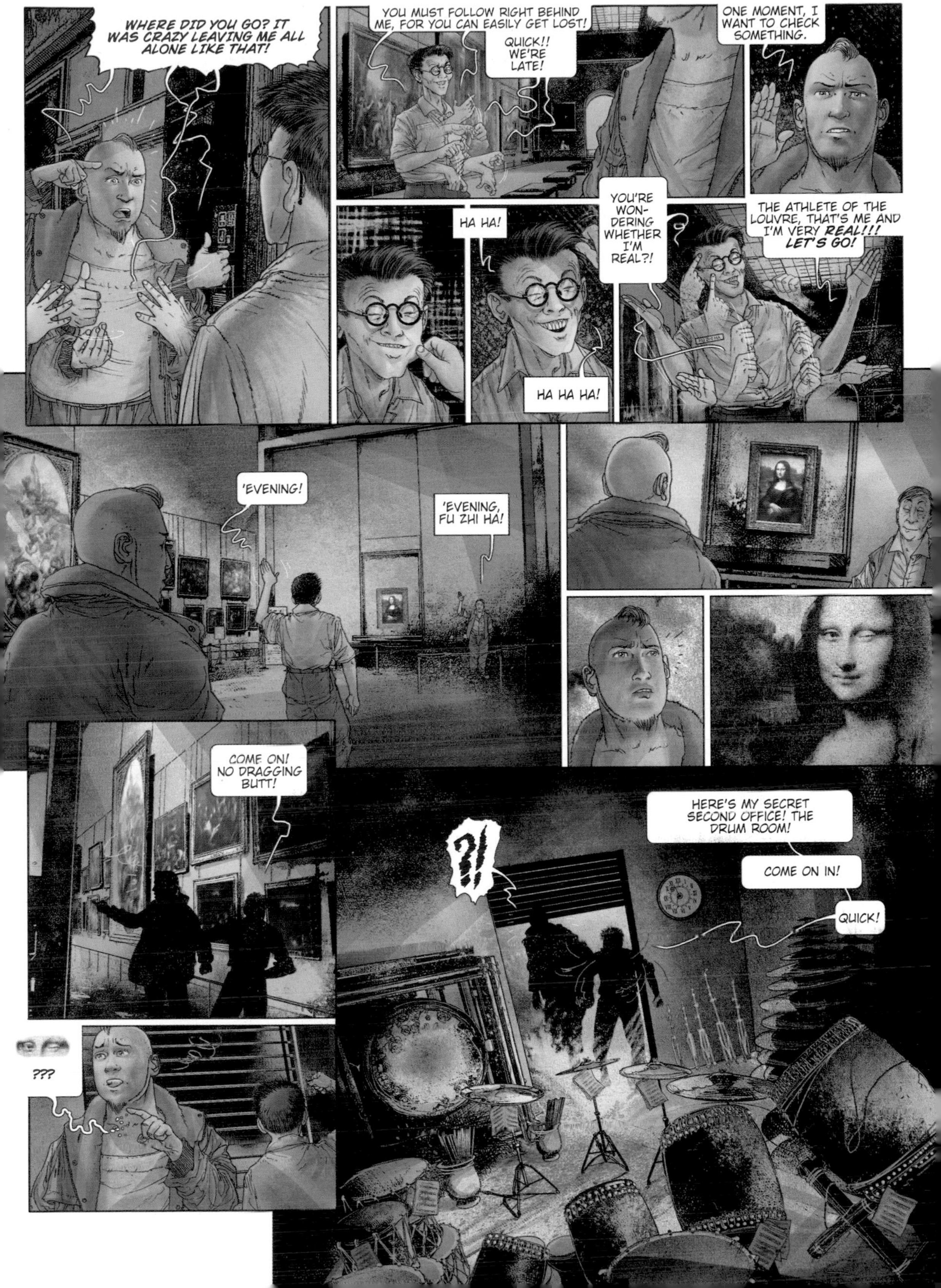
WHERE DID YOU GO? IT WAS CRAZY LEAVING ME ALL ALONE LIKE THAT!
YOU MUST FOLLOW RIGHT BEHIND ME, FOR YOU CAN EASILY GET LOST!
QUICK!! WE'RE LATE!
ONE MOMENT, I WANT TO CHECK SOMETHING.
HA HA!
YOU'RE WON-DERING WHETHER I'M REAL?!
HA HA HA!
THE ATHLETE OF THE LOUVRE, THAT'S ME AND I'M VERY REAL!!! LET'S GO!
'EVENING!
'EVENING, FU ZHI HA!
COME ON! NO DRAGGING BUTT!
???
?!
HERE'S MY SECRET SECOND OFFICE! THE DRUM ROOM!
COME ON IN!
QUICK!

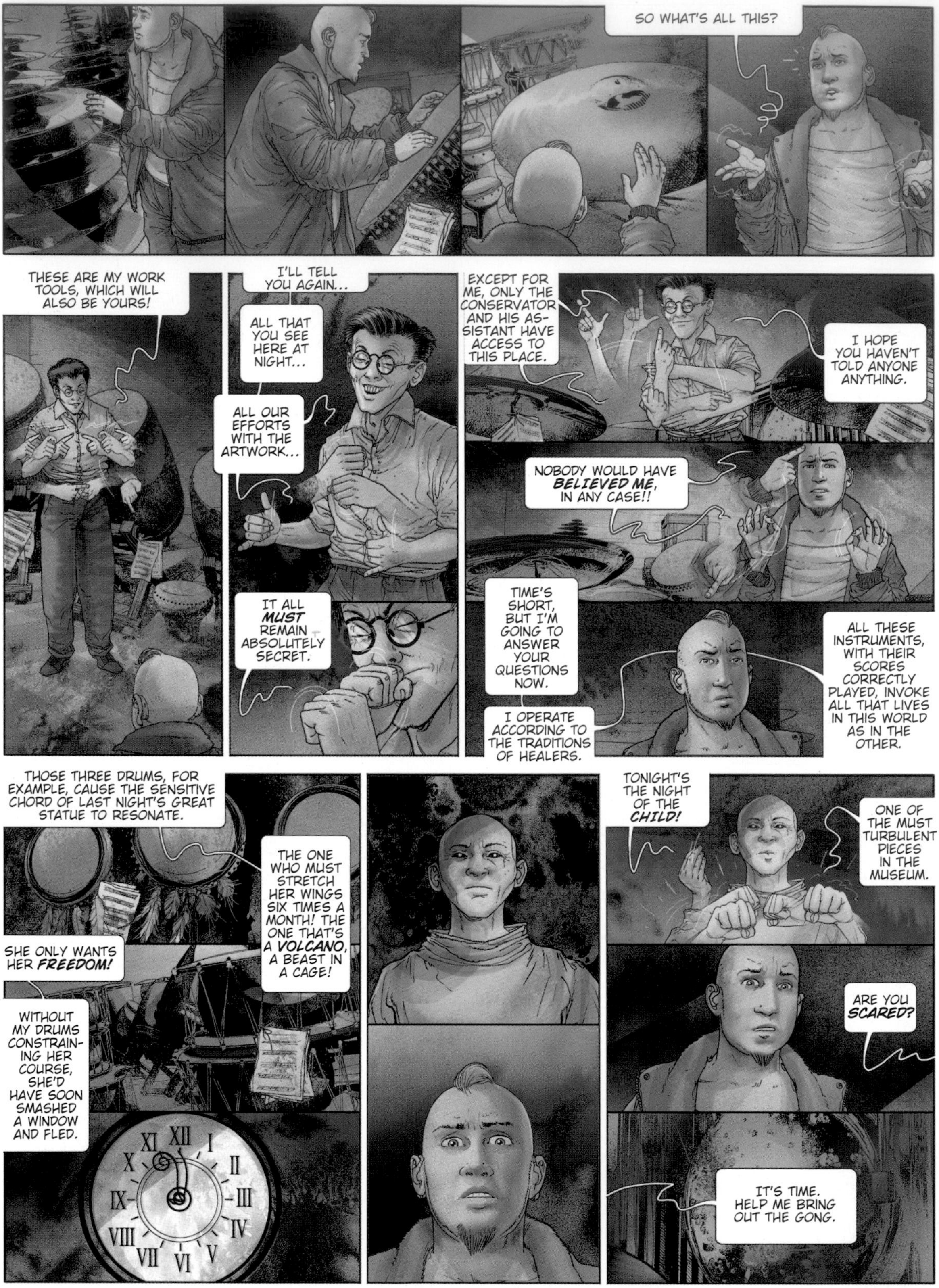

SO WHAT'S ALL THIS?
THESE ARE MY WORK TOOLS, WHICH WILL ALSO BE YOURS!
I'LL TELL YOU AGAIN...
ALL THAT YOU SEE HERE AT NIGHT...
ALL OUR EFFORTS WITH THE ARTWORK...
IT ALL MUST REMAIN ABSOLUTELY SECRET.
EXCEPT FOR ME, ONLY THE CONSERVATOR AND HIS ASSISTANT HAVE ACCESS TO THIS PLACE.
I HOPE YOU HAVEN'T TOLD ANYONE ANYTHING.
NOBODY WOULD HAVE BELIEVED ME, IN ANY CASE!!
TIME'S SHORT, BUT I'M GOING TO ANSWER YOUR QUESTIONS NOW.
I OPERATE ACCORDING TO THE TRADITIONS OF HEALERS.
ALL THESE INSTRUMENTS, WITH THEIR SCORES CORRECTLY PLAYED, INVOKE ALL THAT LIVES IN THIS WORLD AS IN THE OTHER.
THOSE THREE DRUMS, FOR EXAMPLE, CAUSE THE SENSITIVE CHORD OF LAST NIGHT'S GREAT STATUE TO RESONATE.
THE ONE WHO MUST STRETCH HER WINGS SIX TIMES A MONTH! THE ONE THAT'S A VOLCANO, A BEAST IN A CAGE!
SHE ONLY WANTS HER FREEDOM!
WITHOUT MY DRUMS CONSTRAINING HER COURSE, SHE'D HAVE SOON SMASHED A WINDOW AND FLED.
TONIGHT'S THE NIGHT OF THE CHILD!
ONE OF THE MUST TURBULENT PIECES IN THE MUSEUM.
ARE YOU SCARED?
IT'S TIME. HELP ME BRING OUT THE GONG.

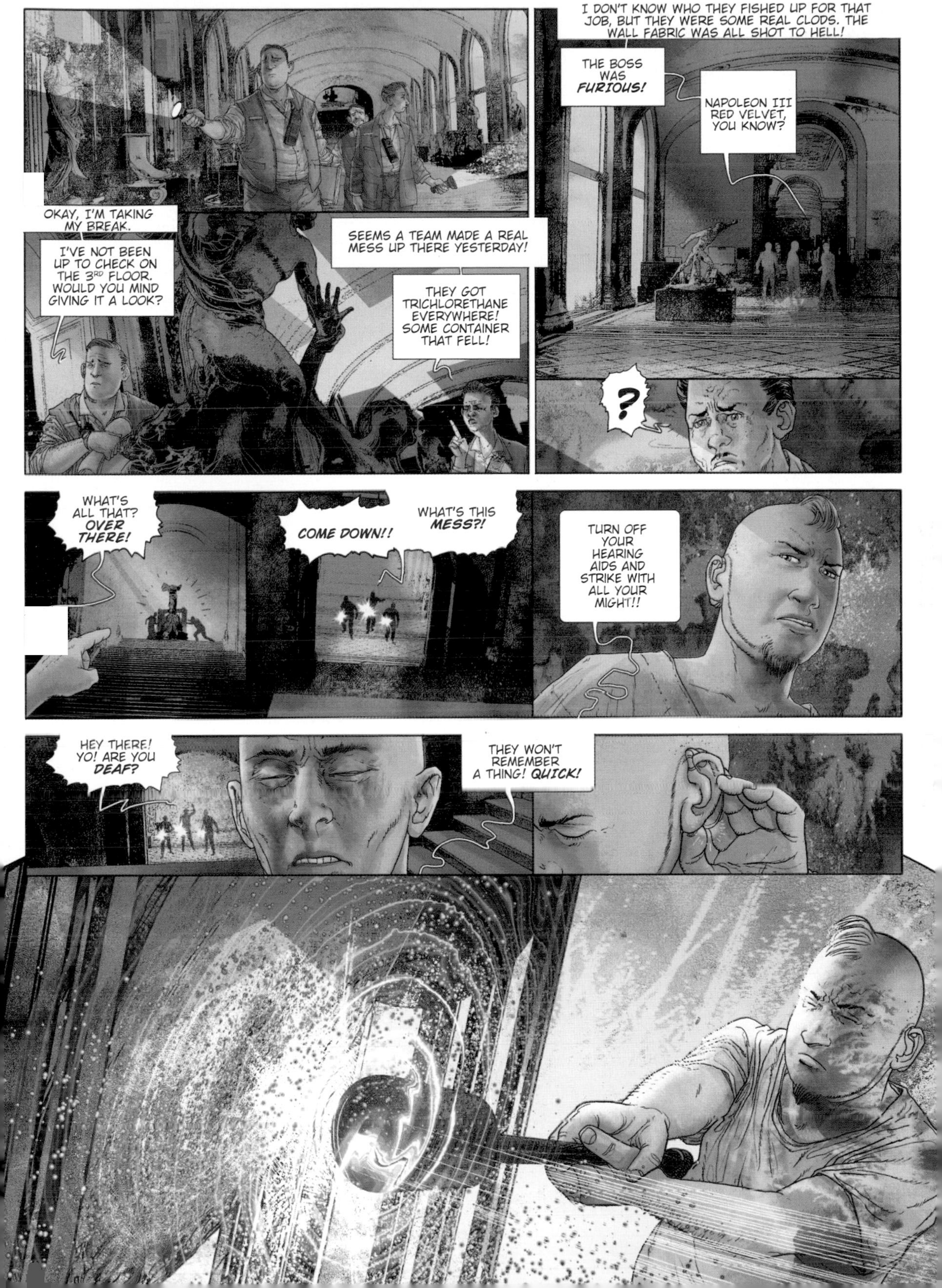
OKAY, I'M TAKING MY BREAK.
I'VE NOT BEEN UP TO CHECK ON THE 3RD FLOOR. WOULD YOU MIND GIVING IT A LOOK?
SEEMS A TEAM MADE A REAL MESS UP THERE YESTERDAY!
THEY GOT TRICHLORETHANE EVERYWHERE! SOME CONTAINER THAT FELL!
I DON'T KNOW WHO THEY FISHED UP FOR THAT JOB, BUT THEY WERE SOME REAL CLODS. THE WALL FABRIC WAS ALL SHOT TO HELL!
THE BOSS WAS FURIOUS!
NAPOLEON III RED VELVET, YOU KNOW?
?
WHAT'S ALL THAT? OVER THERE!
COME DOWN!!
WHAT'S THIS MESS?!
TURN OFF YOUR HEARING AIDS AND STRIKE WITH ALL YOUR MIGHT!!
HEY THERE! YO! ARE YOU DEAF?
THEY WON'T REMEMBER A THING! QUICK!

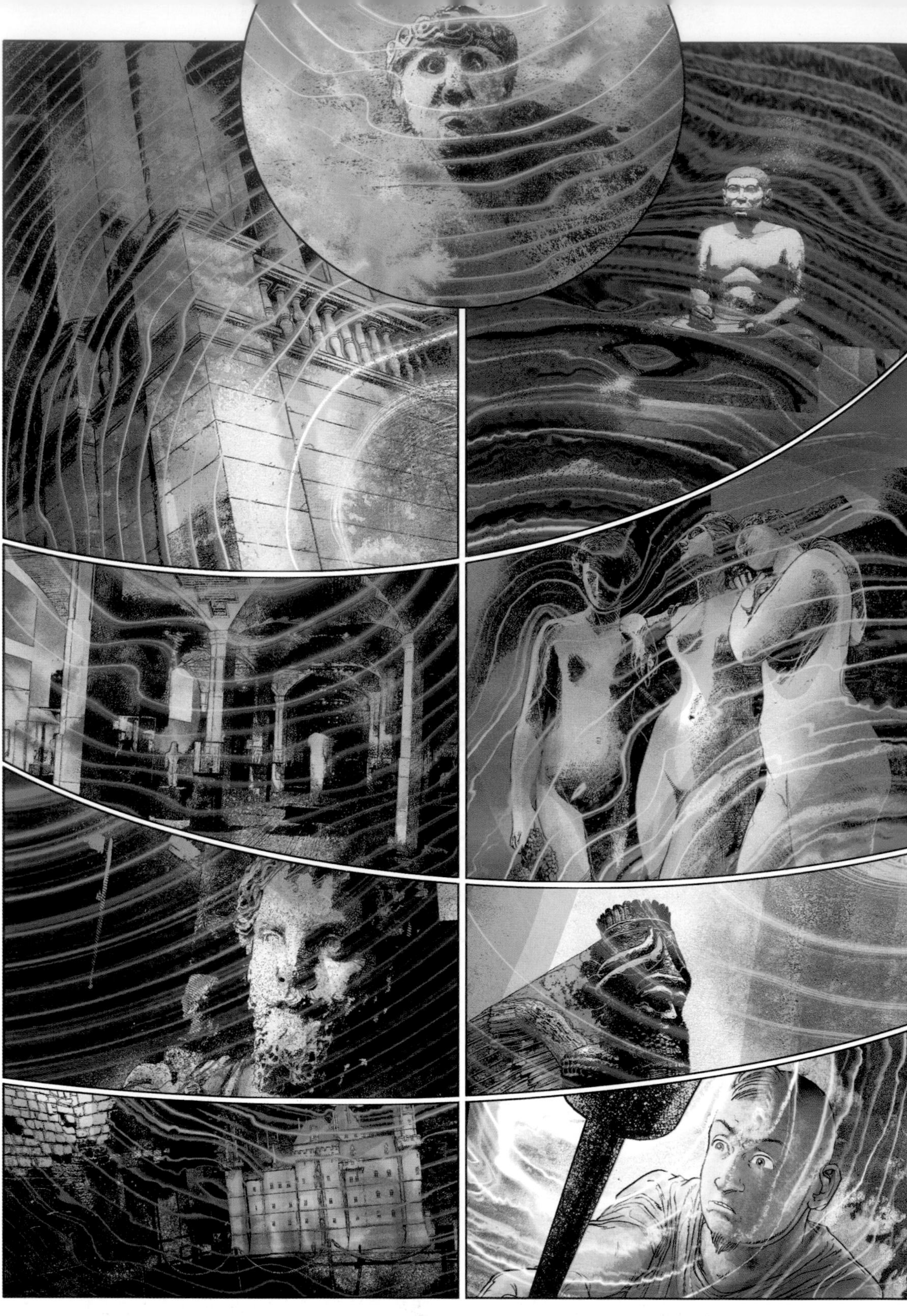

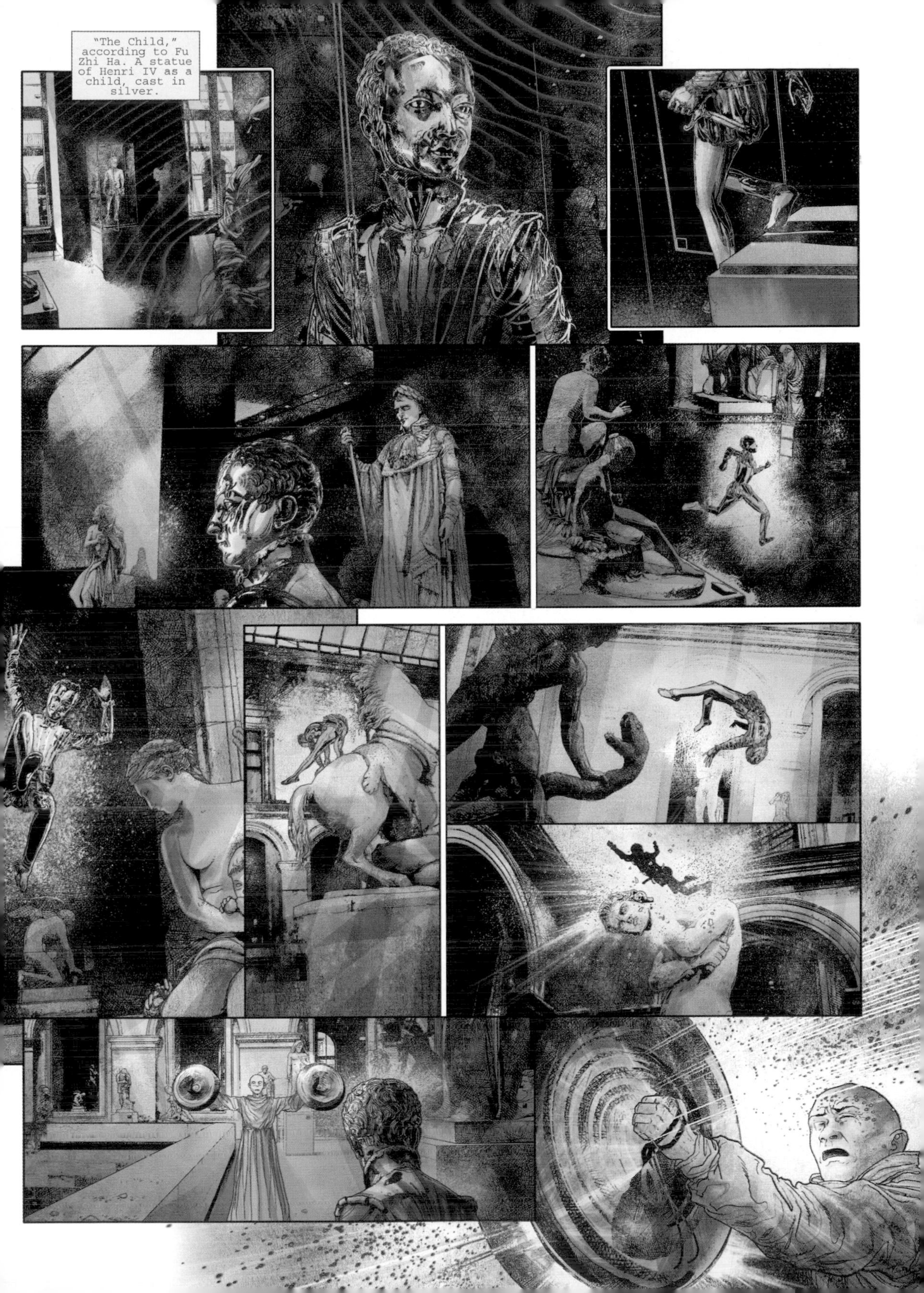
"The Child," according to Fu Zhi Ha. A statue of Henri IV as a child, cast in silver.

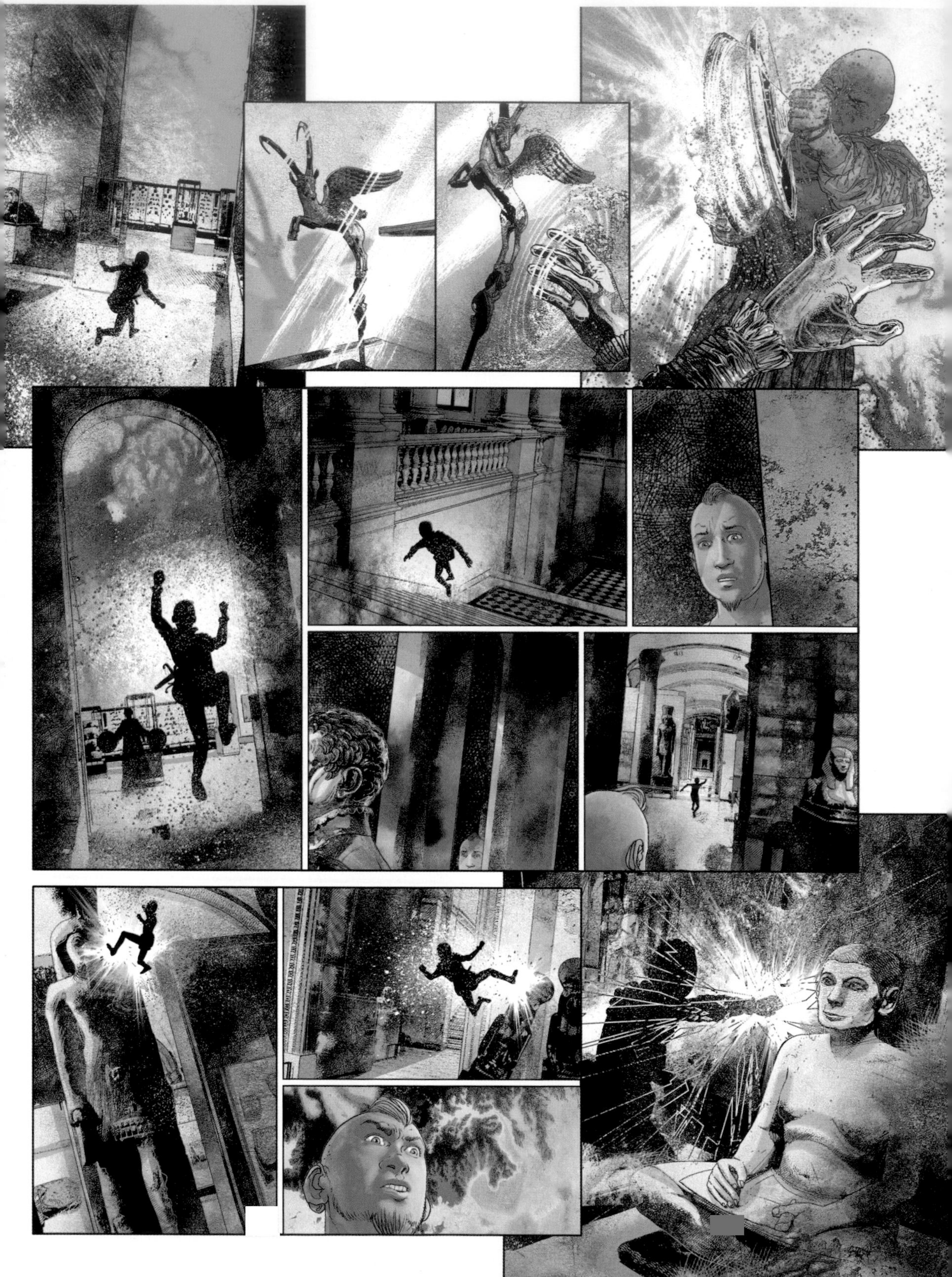

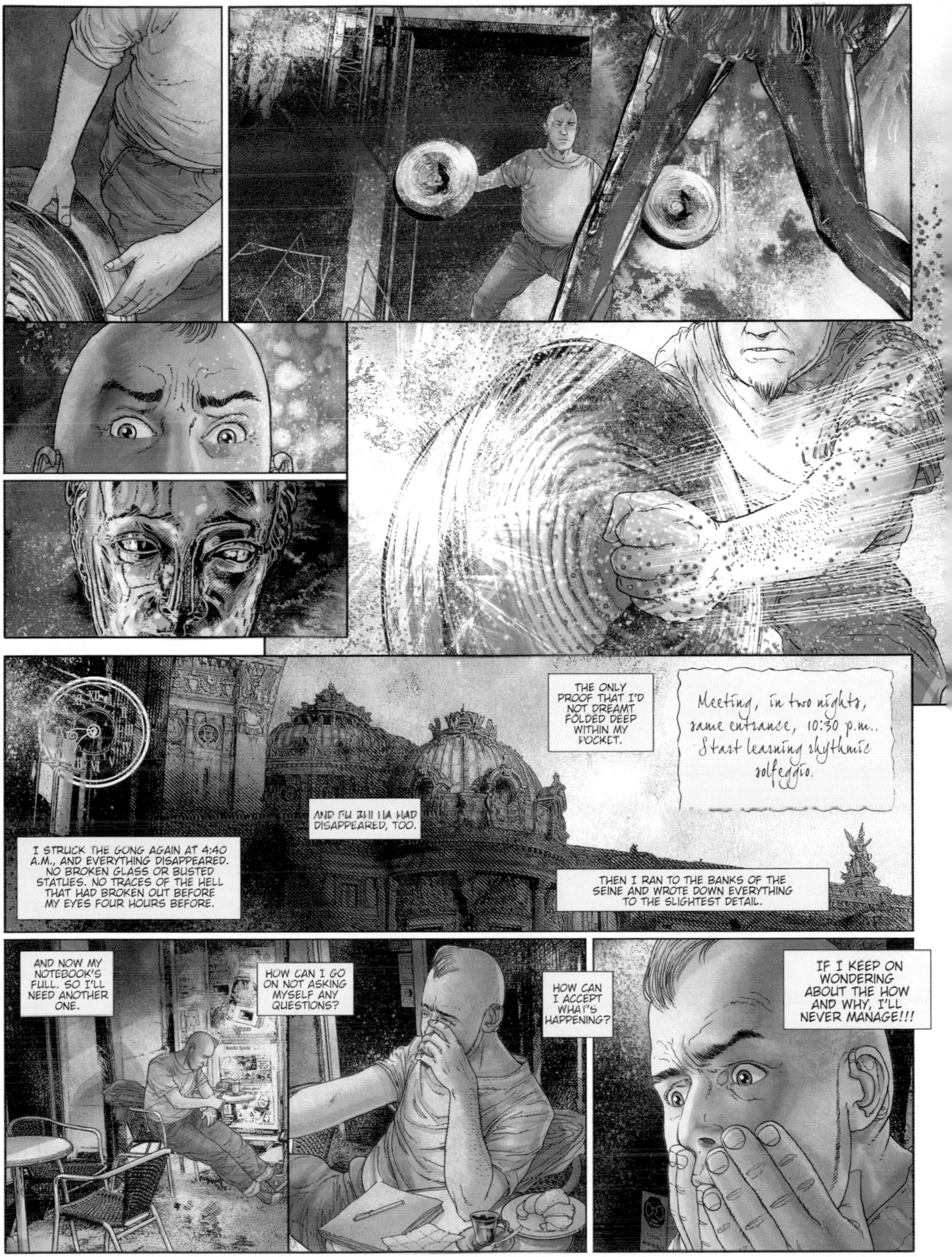
THE ONLY PROOF THAT I'D NOT DREAMT FOLDED DEEP WITHIN MY POCKET.
Meeting, in two nights, same entrance, 10:30 p.m.. Start learning rhythmic solfeggio.
AND HAD DISAPPEARED, TOO.
I STRUCK THE GONG AGAIN AT 4:40 A.M., AND EVERYTHING DISAPPEARED. NO BROKEN GLASS OR BUSTED STATUES. NO TRACES OF THE HELL THAT HAD BROKEN OUT BEFORE MY EYES FOUR HOURS BEFORE.
THEN I RAN TO THE BANKS OF THE SEINE AND WROTE DOWN EVERYTHING TO THE SLIGHTEST DETAIL.
AND NOW MY NOTEBOOK'S FULL. SO I'LL NEED ANOTHER ONE.
HOW CAN I GO ON NOT ASKING MYSELF ANY QUESTIONS?
HOW CAN I ACCEPT WHAT'S HAPPENING?
IF I KEEP ON WONDERING ABOUT THE HOW AND WHY, I'LL NEVER MANAGE!!!

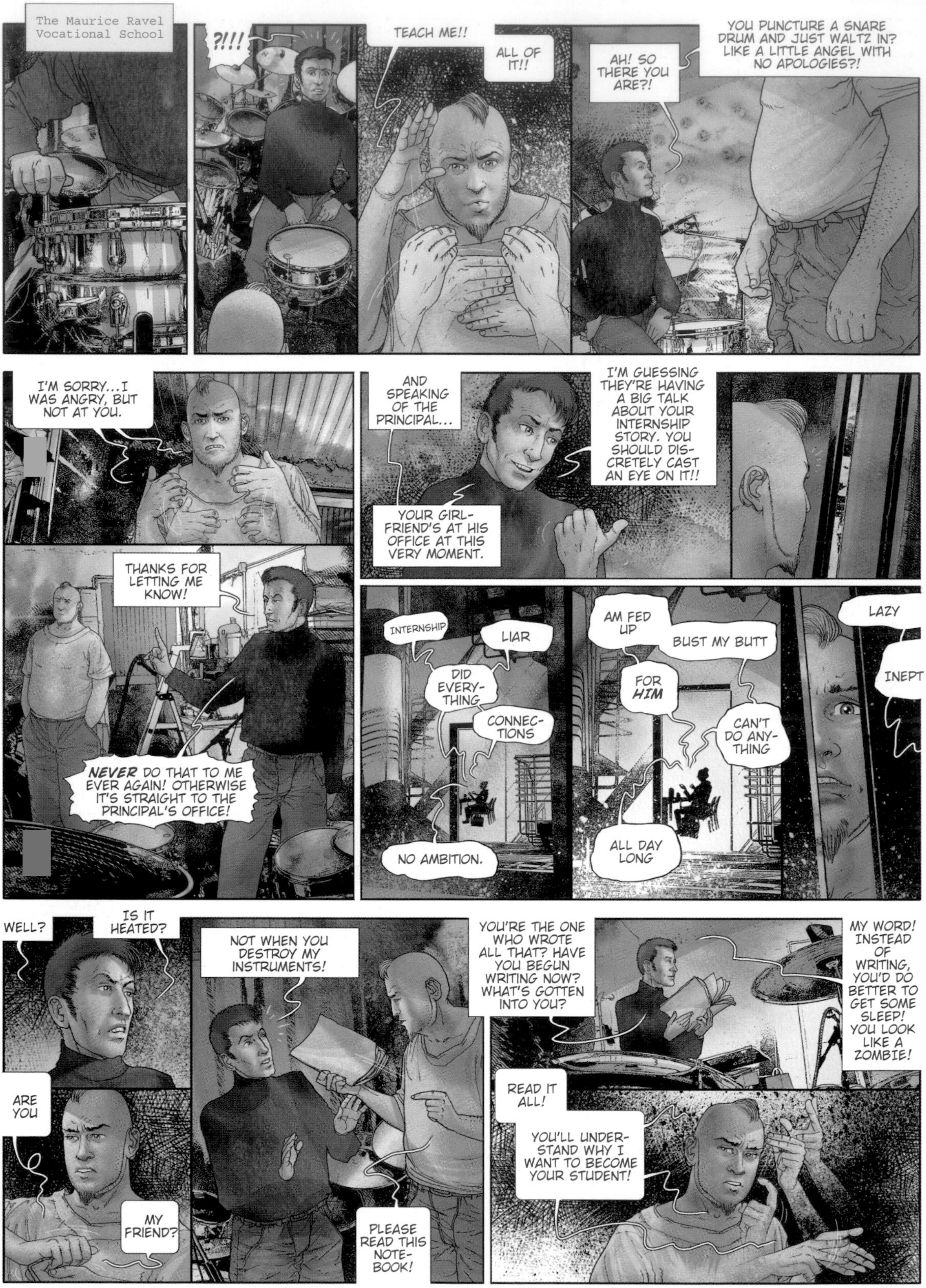

The Maurice Ravel Vocational School
?!!!
TEACH ME!!
ALL OF IT!!
AH! SO THERE YOU ARE?!
YOU PUNCTURE A SNARE DRUM AND JUST WALTZ IN? LIKE A LITTLE ANGEL WITH NO APOLOGIES?!
I'M SORRY... I WAS ANGRY, BUT NOT AT YOU.
THANKS FOR LETTING ME KNOW!
NEVER DO THAT TO ME EVER AGAIN! OTHERWISE IT'S STRAIGHT TO THE PRINCIPAL'S OFFICE!
AND SPEAKING OF THE PRINCIPAL...
YOUR GIRL-FRIEND'S AT HIS OFFICE AT THIS VERY MOMENT.
I'M GUESSING THEY'RE HAVING A BIG TALK ABOUT YOUR INTERNSHIP STORY. YOU SHOULD DIS-CRETELY CAST AN EYE ON IT!!
INTERNSHIP
LIAR
DID EVERY-THING
CONNEC-TIONS
NO AMBITION.
AM FED UP
BUST MY BUTT
FOR HIM
CAN'T DO ANY-THING
ALL DAY LONG
LAZY
INEPT
WELL?
IS IT HEATED?
ARE YOU
MY FRIEND?
NOT WHEN YOU DESTROY MY INSTRUMENTS!
PLEASE READ THIS NOTE-BOOK!
YOU'RE THE ONE WHO WROTE ALL THAT? HAVE YOU BEGUN WRITING NOW? WHAT'S GOTTEN INTO YOU?
MY WORD! INSTEAD OF WRITING, YOU'D DO BETTER TO GET SOME SLEEP! YOU LOOK LIKE A ZOMBIE!
READ IT ALL!
YOU'LL UNDER-STAND WHY I WANT TO BECOME YOUR STUDENT!

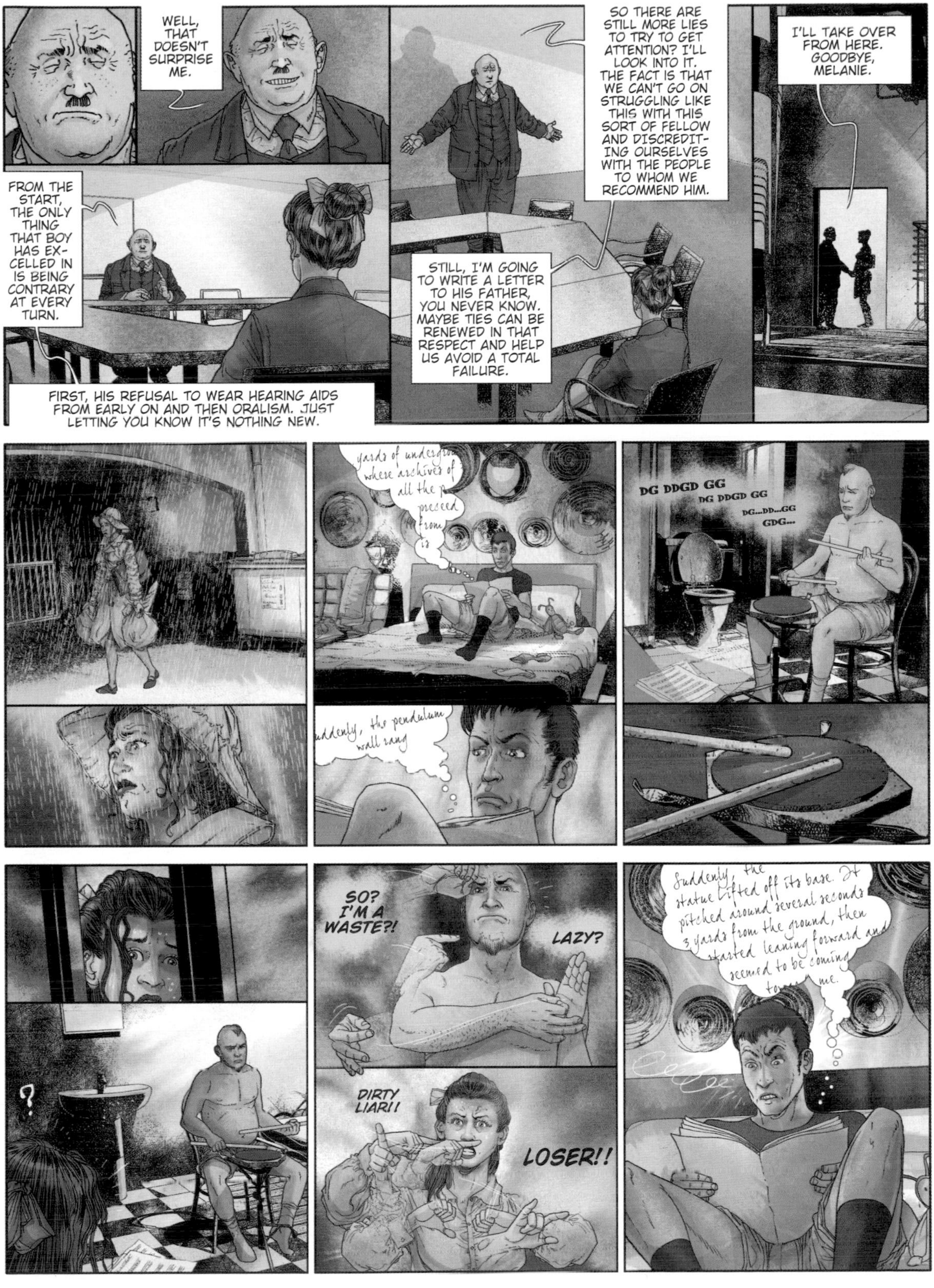

WELL, THAT DOESN'T SURPRISE ME.
FROM THE START, THE ONLY THING THAT BOY HAS EXCELLED IN IS BEING CONTRARY AT EVERY TURN.
FIRST, HIS REFUSAL TO WEAR HEARING AIDS FROM EARLY ON AND THEN ORALISM. JUST LETTING YOU KNOW IT'S NOTHING NEW.
SO THERE ARE STILL MORE LIES TO TRY TO GET ATTENTION? I'LL LOOK INTO IT. THE FACT IS THAT WE CAN'T GO ON STRUGGLING LIKE THIS WITH THIS SORT OF FELLOW AND DISCREDITING OURSELVES WITH THE PEOPLE TO WHOM WE RECOMMEND HIM.
STILL, I'M GOING TO WRITE A LETTER TO HIS FATHER, YOU NEVER KNOW. MAYBE TIES CAN BE RENEWED IN THAT RESPECT AND HELP US AVOID A TOTAL FAILURE.
I'LL TAKE OVER FROM HERE. GOODBYE, MELANIE.
yards of undergro where archives of all the p preceed from is
DG DDGD GG
DG DDGD GG
DG...DD...GG
GDG...
uddenly, the pendulum wall rang
Suddenly, the statue lifted off its base. It pitched around several seconds 3 yards from the ground, then started leaning forward and seemed to be coming to me.
SO? I'M A WASTE?!
LAZY?
?
DIRTY LIAR!!
LOSER!!

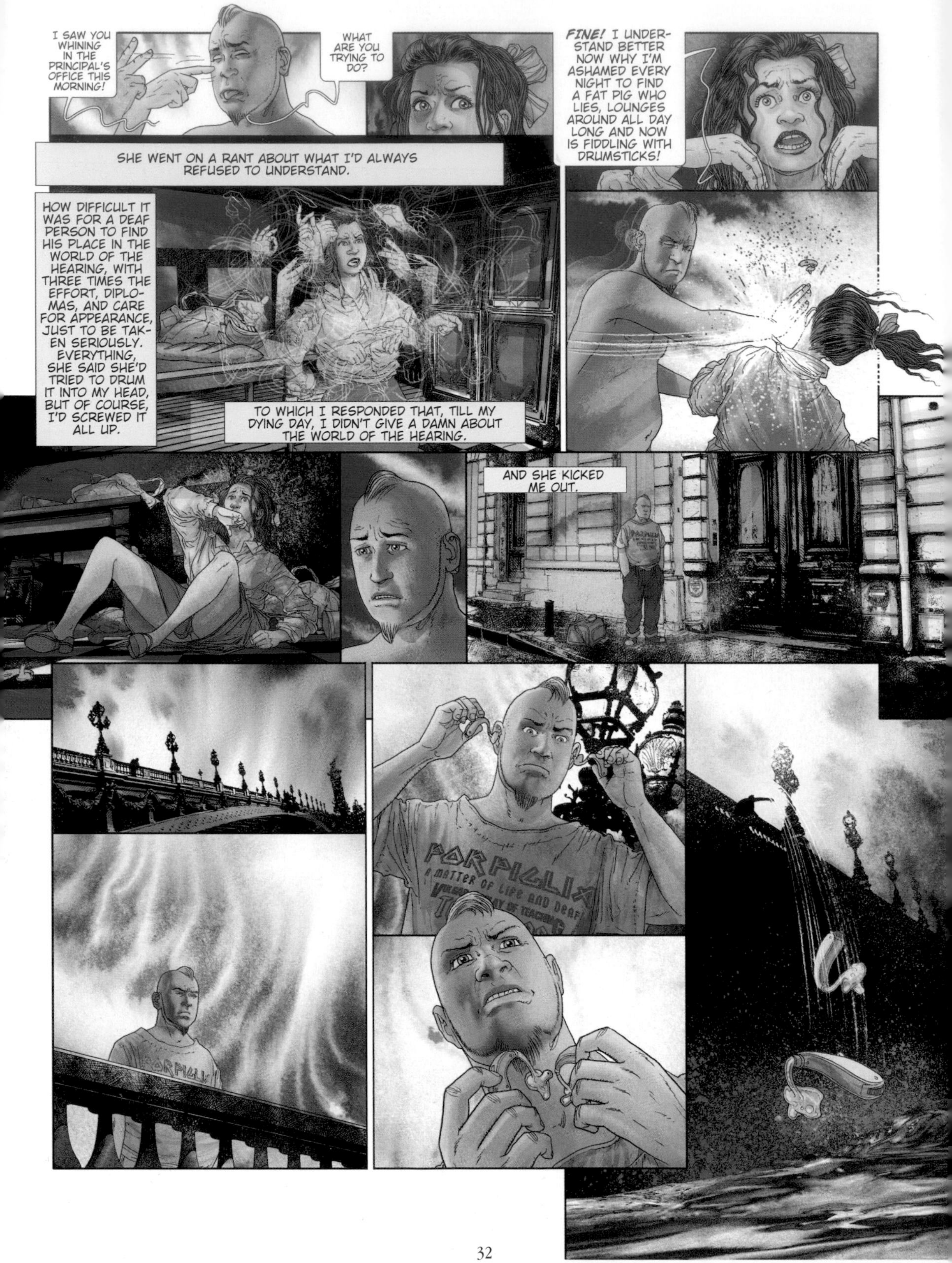
I SAW YOU WHINING IN THE PRINCIPAL'S OFFICE THIS MORNING!
WHAT ARE YOU TRYING TO DO?
FINE! I UNDERSTAND BETTER NOW WHY I'M ASHAMED EVERY NIGHT TO FIND A FAT PIG WHO LIES, LOUNGES AROUND ALL DAY LONG AND NOW IS FIDDLING WITH DRUMSTICKS!
SHE WENT ON A RANT ABOUT WHAT I'D ALWAYS REFUSED TO UNDERSTAND.
HOW DIFFICULT IT WAS FOR A DEAF PERSON TO FIND HIS PLACE IN THE WORLD OF THE HEARING, WITH THREE TIMES THE EFFORT, DIPLOMAS, AND CARE FOR APPEARANCE, JUST TO BE TAKEN SERIOUSLY. EVERYTHING, SHE SAID SHE'D TRIED TO DRUM IT INTO MY HEAD, BUT OF COURSE, I'D SCREWED IT ALL UP.
TO WHICH I RESPONDED THAT, TILL MY DYING DAY, I DIDN'T GIVE A DAMN ABOUT THE WORLD OF THE HEARING.
AND SHE KICKED ME OUT.
PORPIGLIA
A MATTER OF LIFE AND DEAF

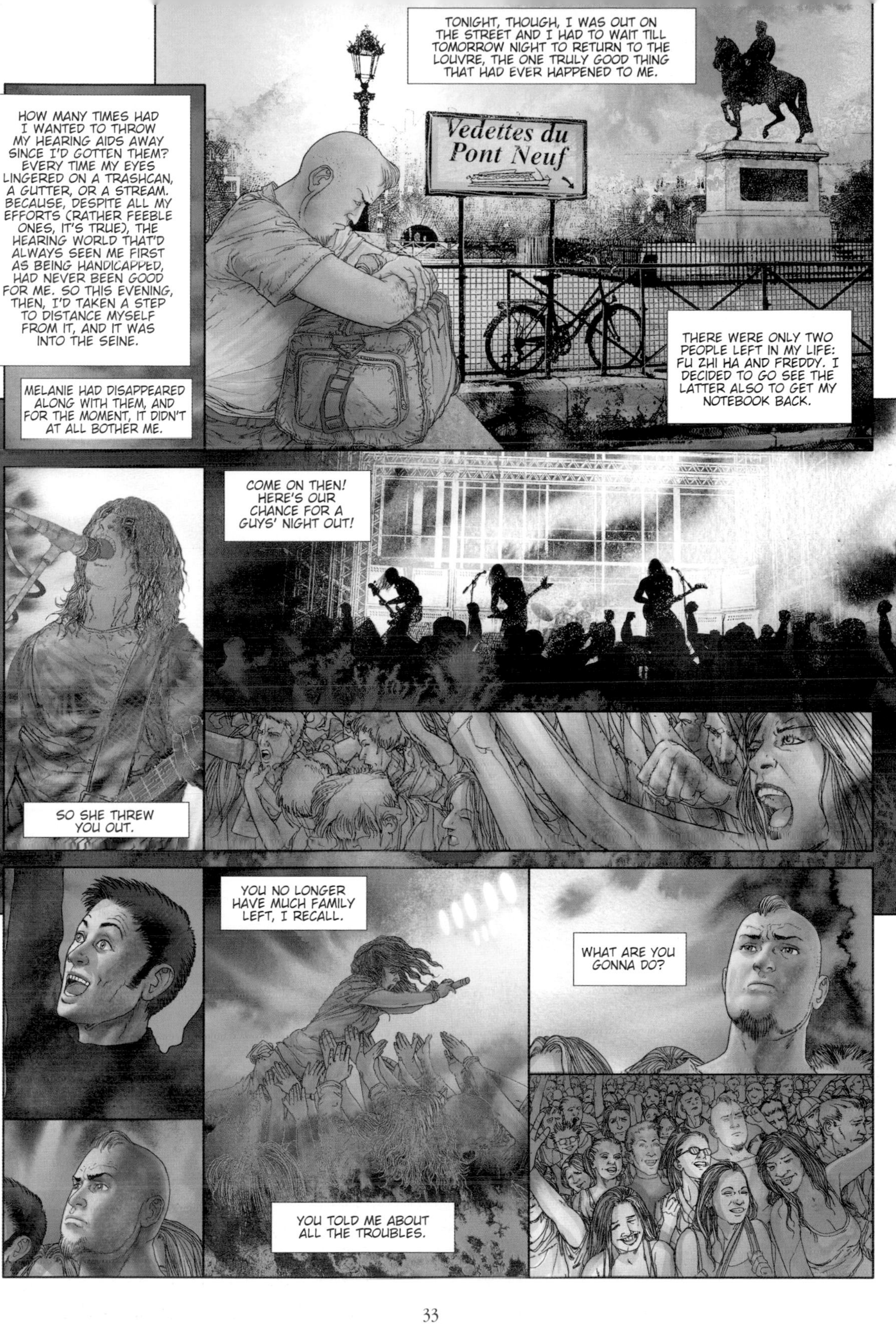
TONIGHT, THOUGH, I WAS OUT ON THE STREET AND I HAD TO WAIT TILL TOMORROW NIGHT TO RETURN TO THE LOUVRE, THE ONE TRULY GOOD THING THAT HAD EVER HAPPENED TO ME.
HOW MANY TIMES HAD I WANTED TO THROW MY HEARING AIDS AWAY SINCE I'D GOTTEN THEM? EVERY TIME MY EYES LINGERED ON A TRASHCAN, A GUTTER, OR A STREAM. BECAUSE, DESPITE ALL MY EFFORTS (RATHER FEEBLE ONES, IT'S TRUE), THE HEARING WORLD THAT'D ALWAYS SEEN ME FIRST AS BEING HANDICAPPED, HAD NEVER BEEN GOOD FOR ME. SO THIS EVENING, THEN, I'D TAKEN A STEP TO DISTANCE MYSELF FROM IT, AND IT WAS INTO THE SEINE.
Vedettes du Pont Neuf
MELANIE HAD DISAPPEARED ALONG WITH THEM, AND FOR THE MOMENT, IT DIDN'T AT ALL BOTHER ME.
THERE WERE ONLY TWO PEOPLE LEFT IN MY LIFE: FU ZHI HA AND FREDDY. I DECIDED TO GO SEE THE LATTER ALSO TO GET MY NOTEBOOK BACK.
COME ON THEN! HERE'S OUR CHANCE FOR A GUYS' NIGHT OUT!
SO SHE THREW YOU OUT.
YOU NO LONGER HAVE MUCH FAMILY LEFT, I RECALL.
YOU TOLD ME ABOUT ALL THE TROUBLES.
WHAT ARE YOU GONNA DO?

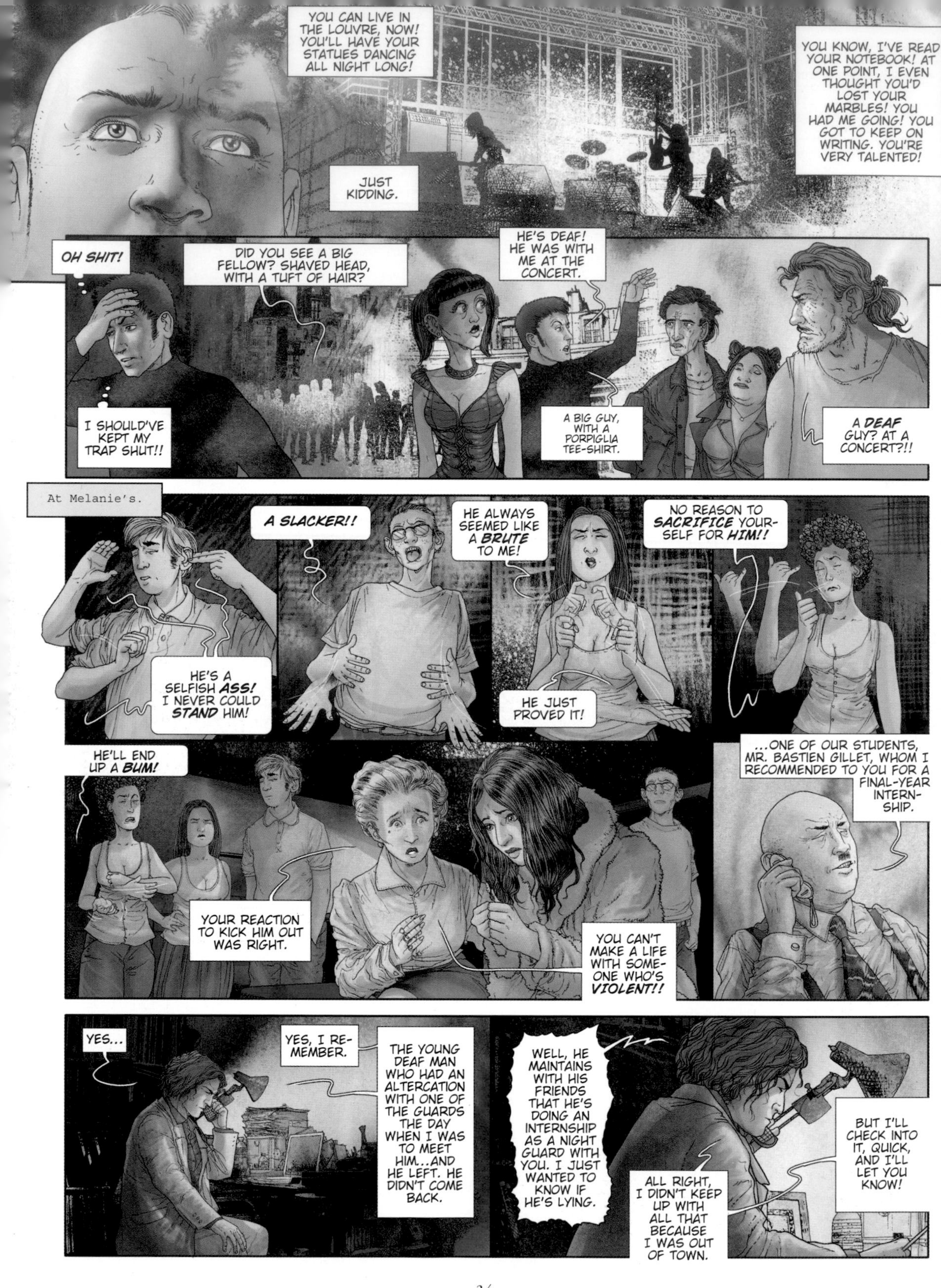

YOU CAN LIVE IN THE LOUVRE, NOW! YOU'LL HAVE YOUR STATUES DANCING ALL NIGHT LONG!
JUST KIDDING.
YOU KNOW, I'VE READ YOUR NOTEBOOK! AT ONE POINT, I EVEN THOUGHT YOU'D LOST YOUR MARBLES! YOU HAD ME GOING! YOU GOT TO KEEP ON WRITING. YOU'RE VERY TALENTED!
OH SHIT!
I SHOULD'VE KEPT MY TRAP SHUT!!
DID YOU SEE A BIG FELLOW? SHAVED HEAD, WITH A TUFT OF HAIR?
HE'S DEAF! HE WAS WITH ME AT THE CONCERT.
A BIG GUY, WITH A PORPIGLIA TEE-SHIRT.
A DEAF GUY? AT A CONCERT?!!
At Melanie's.
HE'S A SELFISH ASS! I NEVER COULD STAND HIM!
A SLACKER!!
HE ALWAYS SEEMED LIKE A BRUTE TO ME!
HE JUST PROVED IT!
NO REASON TO SACRIFICE YOURSELF FOR HIM!!
HE'LL END UP A BUM!
YOUR REACTION TO KICK HIM OUT WAS RIGHT.
YOU CAN'T MAKE A LIFE WITH SOMEONE WHO'S VIOLENT!!
...ONE OF OUR STUDENTS, MR. BASTIEN GILLET, WHOM I RECOMMENDED TO YOU FOR A FINAL-YEAR INTERNSHIP.
YES...
YES, I REMEMBER.
THE YOUNG DEAF MAN WHO HAD AN ALTERCATION WITH ONE OF THE GUARDS THE DAY WHEN I WAS TO MEET HIM...AND HE LEFT. HE DIDN'T COME BACK.
WELL, HE MAINTAINS WITH HIS FRIENDS THAT HE'S DOING AN INTERNSHIP AS A NIGHT GUARD WITH YOU. I JUST WANTED TO KNOW IF HE'S LYING.
ALL RIGHT, I DIDN'T KEEP UP WITH ALL THAT BECAUSE I WAS OUT OF TOWN.
BUT I'LL CHECK INTO IT, QUICK, AND I'LL LET YOU KNOW!

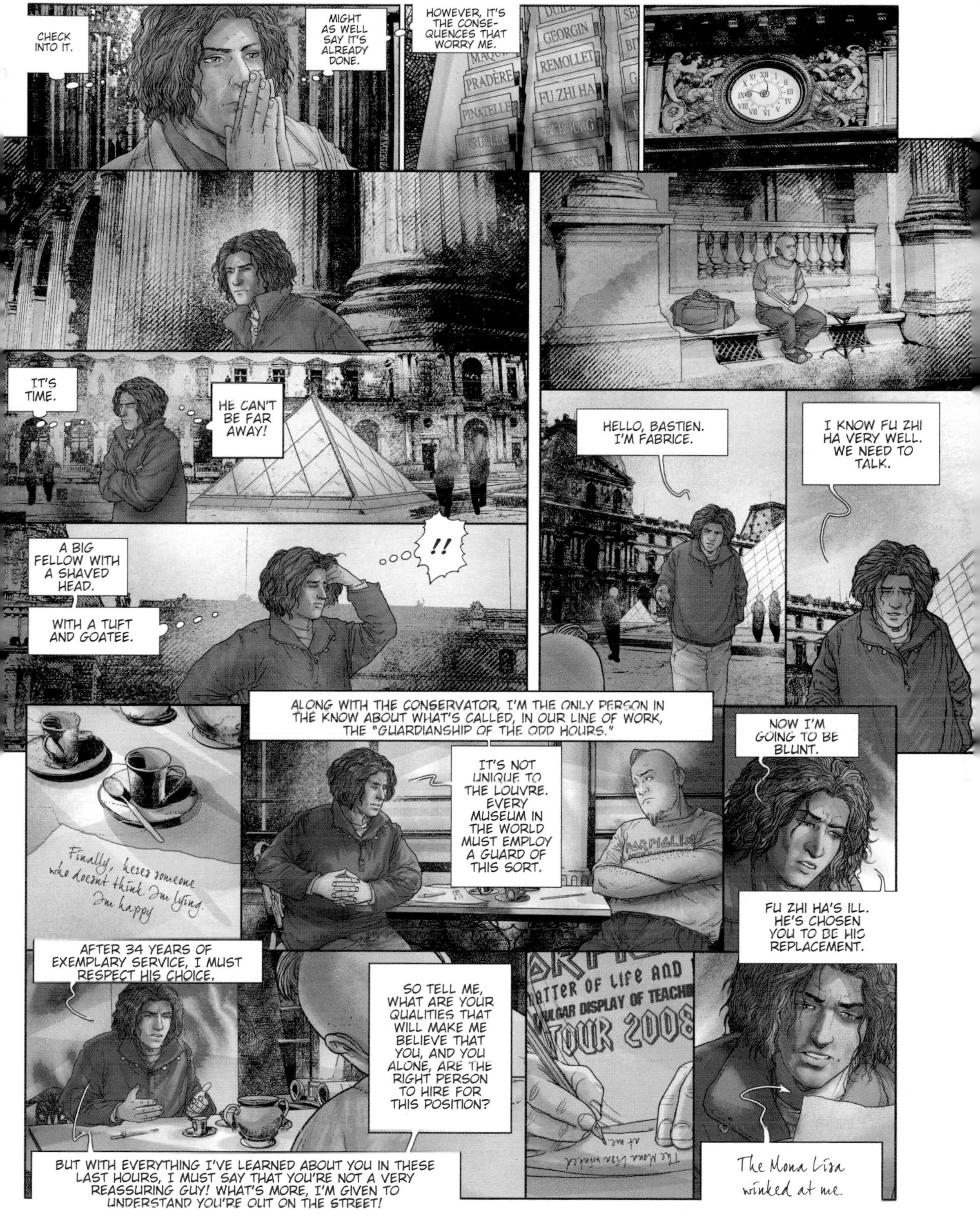
CHECK INTO IT.
MIGHT AS WELL SAY IT'S ALREADY DONE.
HOWEVER, IT'S THE CONSE-QUENCES THAT WORRY ME.
PRADÈRE
PINATELLE
GEORGIN
REMOLLET
FU ZHI HA
IT'S TIME.
HE CAN'T BE FAR AWAY!
A BIG FELLOW WITH A SHAVED HEAD.
WITH A TUFT AND GOATEE.
!!
HELLO, BASTIEN. I'M FABRICE.
I KNOW FU ZHI HA VERY WELL. WE NEED TO TALK.
ALONG WITH THE CONSERVATOR, I'M THE ONLY PERSON IN THE KNOW ABOUT WHAT'S CALLED, IN OUR LINE OF WORK, THE "GUARDIANSHIP OF THE ODD HOURS."
IT'S NOT UNIQUE TO THE LOUVRE. EVERY MUSEUM IN THE WORLD MUST EMPLOY A GUARD OF THIS SORT.
NOW I'M GOING TO BE BLUNT.
Finally, here's someone who doesn't think I'm lying. I'm happy
FU ZHI HA'S ILL. HE'S CHOSEN YOU TO BE HIS REPLACEMENT.
AFTER 34 YEARS OF EXEMPLARY SERVICE, I MUST RESPECT HIS CHOICE.
SO TELL ME, WHAT ARE YOUR QUALITIES THAT WILL MAKE ME BELIEVE THAT YOU, AND YOU ALONE, ARE THE RIGHT PERSON TO HIRE FOR THIS POSITION?
TOUR 2008
BUT WITH EVERYTHING I'VE LEARNED ABOUT YOU IN THESE LAST HOURS, I MUST SAY THAT YOU'RE NOT A VERY REASSURING GUY! WHAT'S MORE, I'M GIVEN TO UNDERSTAND YOU'RE OUT ON THE STREET!
The Mona Lisa winked at me.

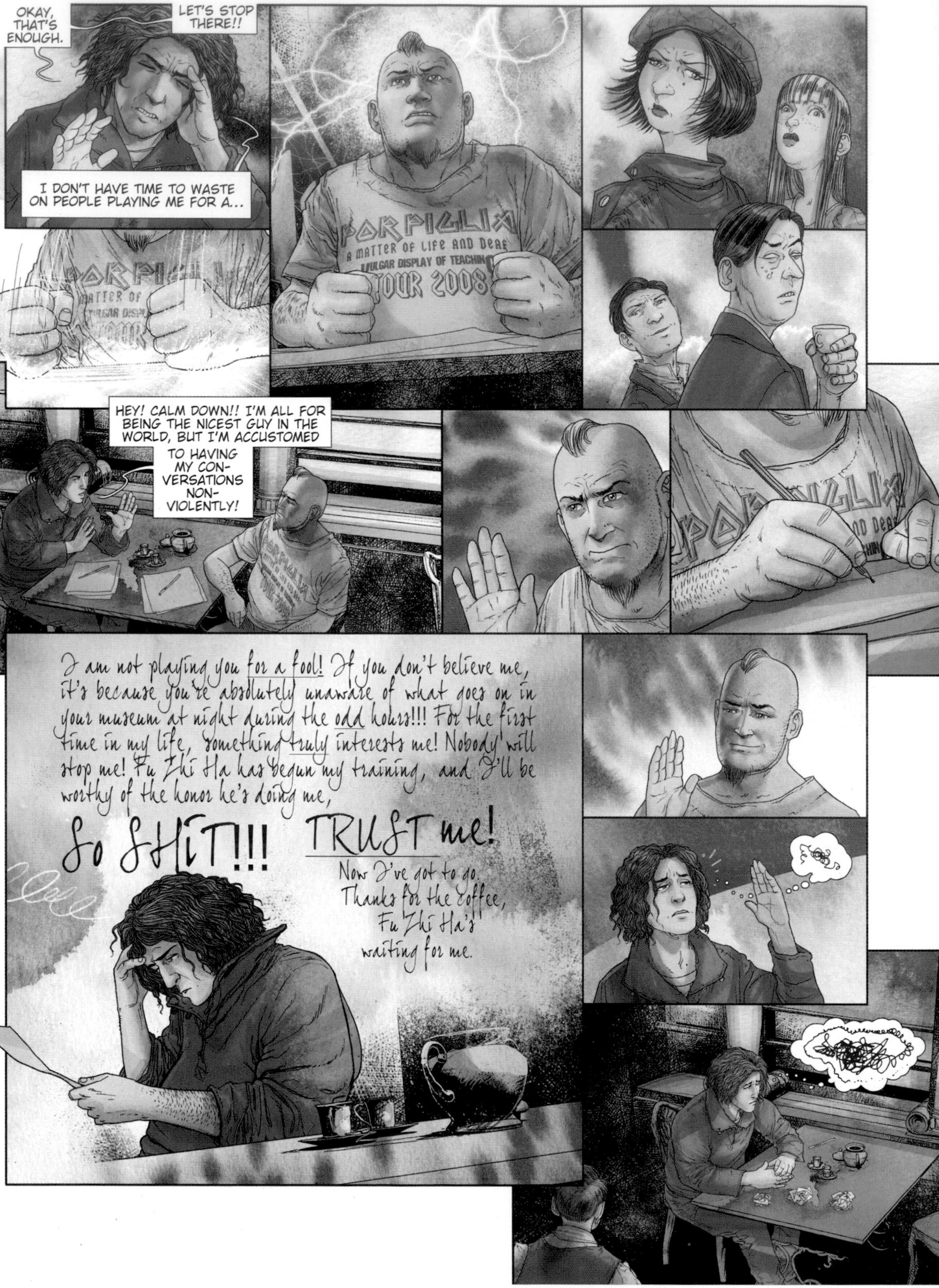

OKAY, THAT'S ENOUGH.
LET'S STOP THERE!!
I DON'T HAVE TIME TO WASTE ON PEOPLE PLAYING ME FOR A...
PORPIGLIA
A MATTER OF LIFE AND DEAF
VULGAR DISPLAY OF TEACHING
TOUR 2008
HEY! CALM DOWN!! I'M ALL FOR BEING THE NICEST GUY IN THE WORLD, BUT I'M ACCUSTOMED
TO HAVING MY CONVERSATIONS NON-VIOLENTLY!
I am not playing you for a fool! If you don't believe me, it's because you're absolutely unaware of what goes on in your museum at night during the odd hours!!! For the first time in my life, something truly interests me! Nobody will stop me! Fu Zhi Ha has begun my training, and I'll be worthy of the honor he's doing me,
So SHIT!!! TRUST me!
Now I've got to go. Thanks for the coffee, Fu Zhi Ha's waiting for me.

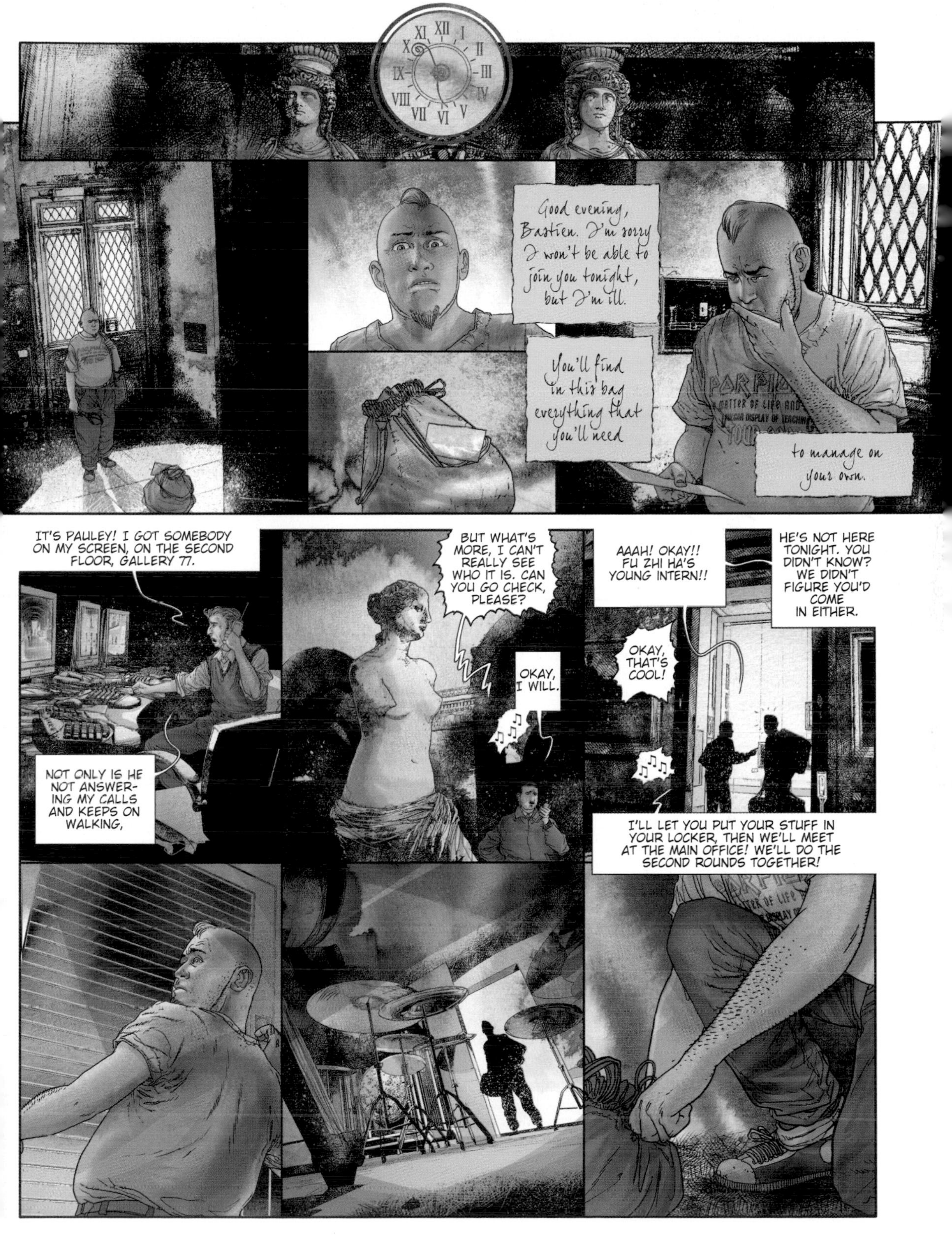

Good evening, Bastien. I'm sorry I won't be able to join you tonight, but I'm ill.
You'll find in this bag everything that you'll need
to manage on your own.
IT'S PAULEY! I GOT SOMEBODY ON MY SCREEN, ON THE SECOND FLOOR, GALLERY 77.
NOT ONLY IS HE NOT ANSWERING MY CALLS AND KEEPS ON WALKING,
BUT WHAT'S MORE, I CAN'T REALLY SEE WHO IT IS. CAN YOU GO CHECK, PLEASE?
OKAY, I WILL.
AAAH! OKAY!! FU ZHI HA'S YOUNG INTERN!!
HE'S NOT HERE TONIGHT. YOU DIDN'T KNOW? WE DIDN'T FIGURE YOU'D COME IN EITHER.
OKAY, THAT'S COOL!
I'LL LET YOU PUT YOUR STUFF IN YOUR LOCKER, THEN WE'LL MEET AT THE MAIN OFFICE! WE'LL DO THE SECOND ROUNDS TOGETHER!

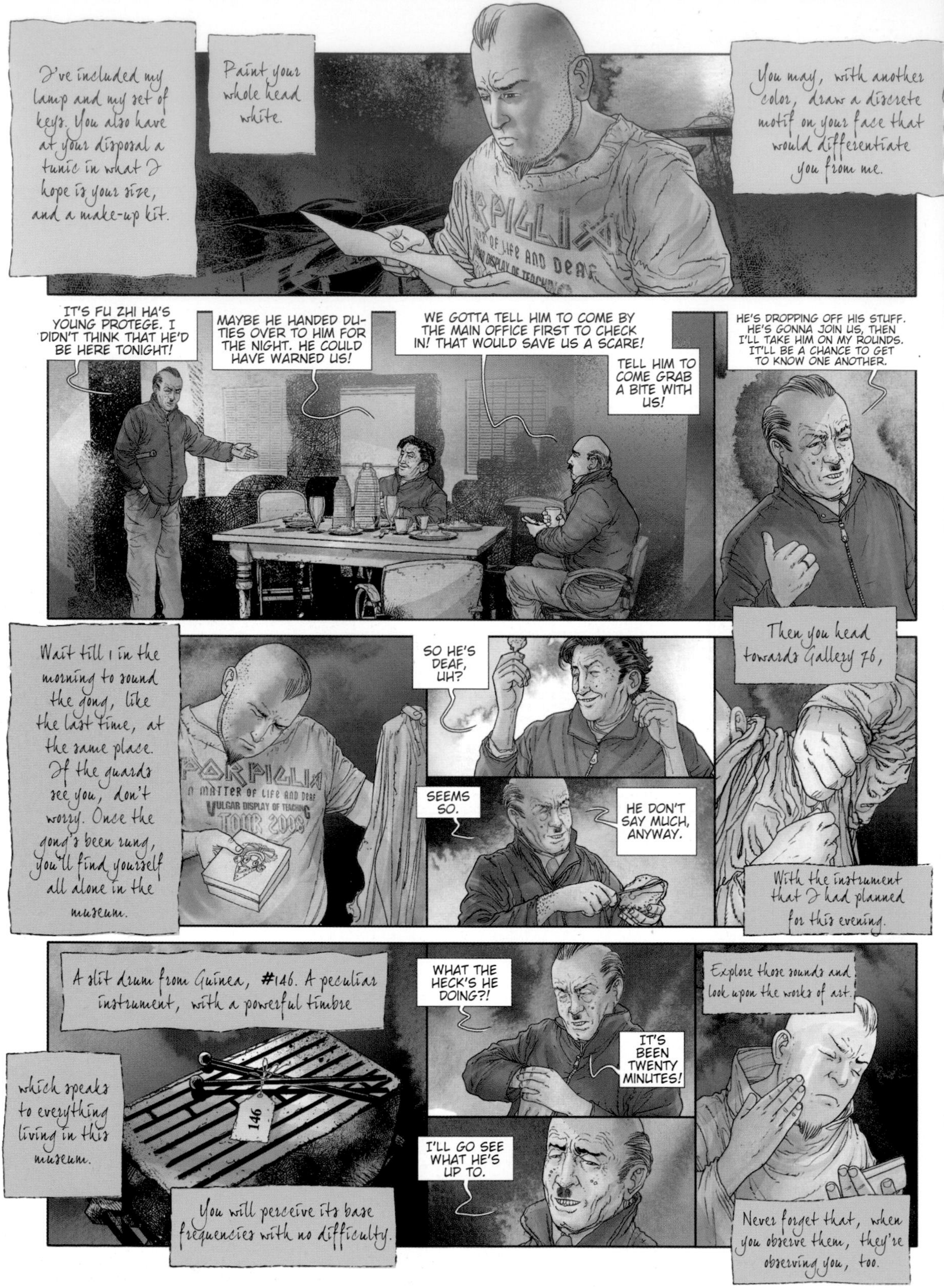

I've included my lamp and my set of keys. You also have at your disposal a tunic in what I hope is your size, and a make-up kit.
Paint your whole head white.
You may, with another color, draw a discrete motif on your face that would differentiate you from me.
IT'S FU ZHI HA'S YOUNG PROTEGE. I DIDN'T THINK THAT HE'D BE HERE TONIGHT!
MAYBE HE HANDED DUTIES OVER TO HIM FOR THE NIGHT. HE COULD HAVE WARNED US!
WE GOTTA TELL HIM TO COME BY THE MAIN OFFICE FIRST TO CHECK IN! THAT WOULD SAVE US A SCARE!
TELL HIM TO COME GRAB A BITE WITH US!
HE'S DROPPING OFF HIS STUFF. HE'S GONNA JOIN US, THEN I'LL TAKE HIM ON MY ROUNDS. IT'LL BE A CHANCE TO GET TO KNOW ONE ANOTHER.
Wait till 1 in the morning to sound the gong, like the last time, at the same place. If the guards see you, don't worry. Once the gong's been rung, you'll find yourself all alone in the museum.
SO HE'S DEAF, UH?
SEEMS SO.
HE DON'T SAY MUCH, ANYWAY.
Then you head towards Gallery 76,
With the instrument that I had planned for this evening.
A slit drum from Guinea, #146. A peculiar instrument, with a powerful timbre
which speaks to everything living in this museum.
146
You will perceive its base frequencies with no difficulty.
WHAT THE HECK'S HE DOING?!
IT'S BEEN TWENTY MINUTES!
I'LL GO SEE WHAT HE'S UP TO.
Explore those sounds and look upon the works of art.
Never forget that, when you observe them, they're observing you, too.

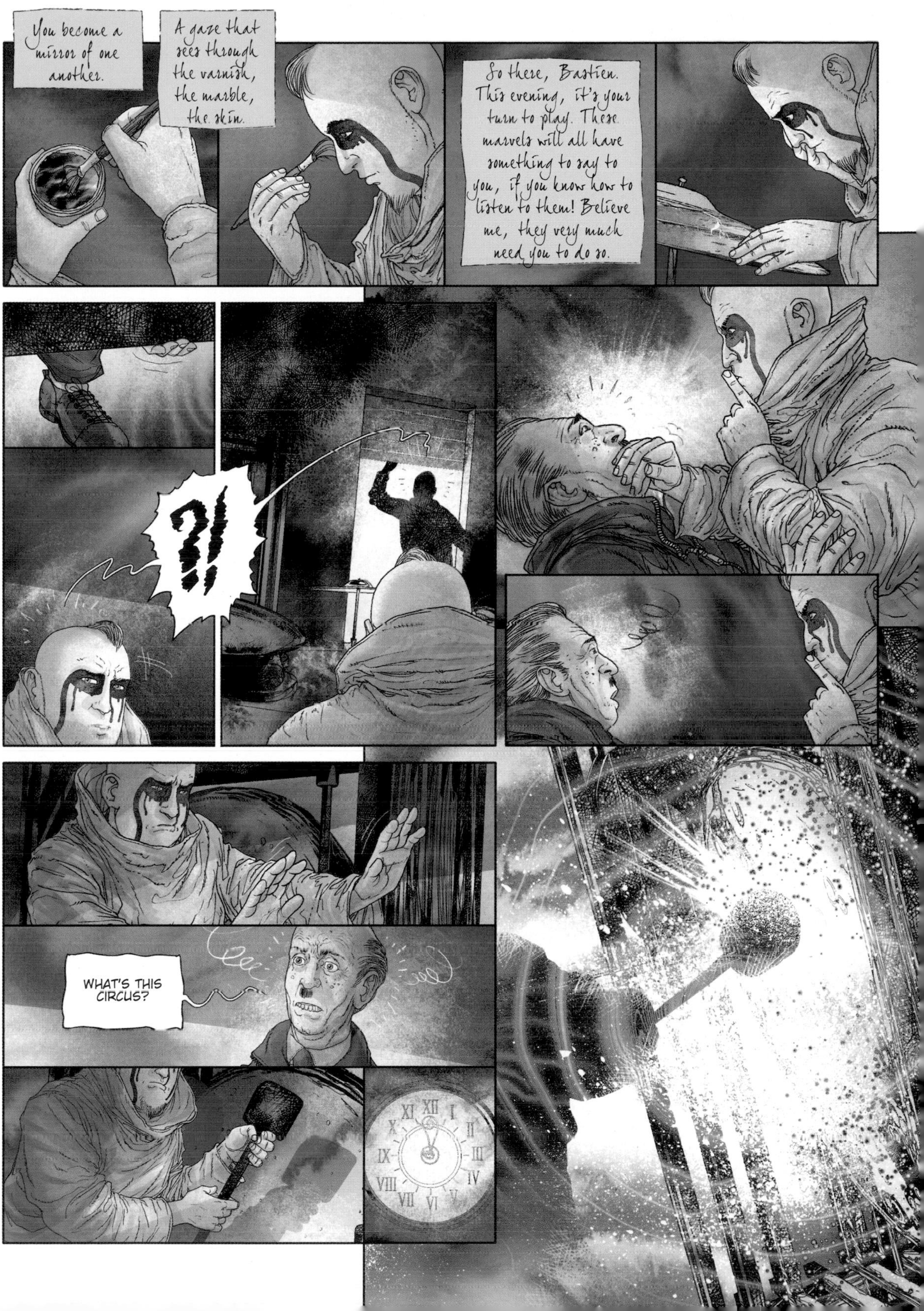
You become a mirror of one another.
A gaze that sees through the varnish, the marble, the skin.
So there, Bastien. This evening, it's your turn to play. These marvels will all have something to say to you, if you know how to listen to them! Believe me, they very much need you to do so.
?!
WHAT'S THIS CIRCUS?

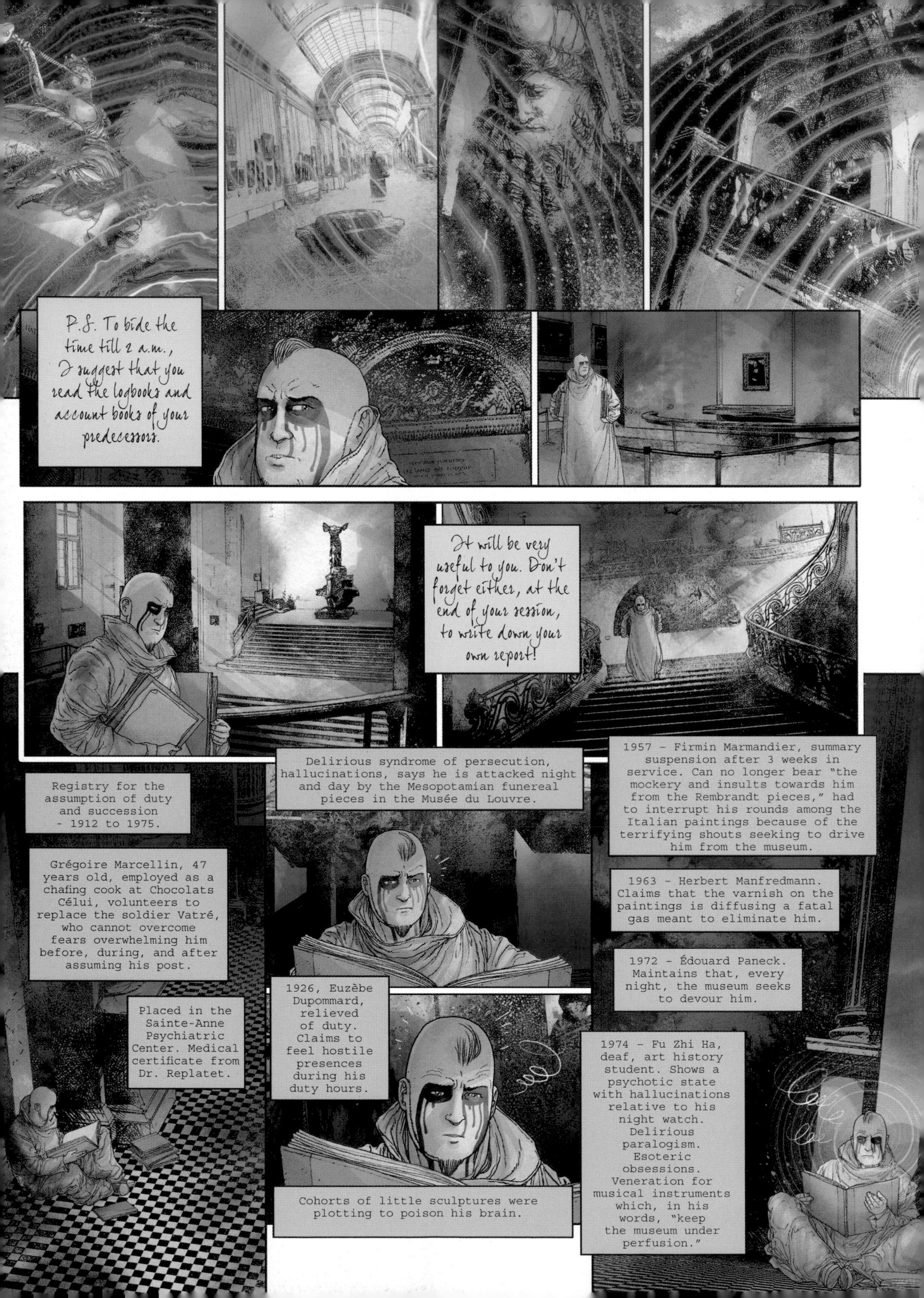
P.S. To bide the time till 2 a.m., I suggest that you read the logbooks and account books of your predecessors.
It will be very useful to you. Don't forget either, at the end of your session, to write down your own report!
Registry for the assumption of duty and succession - 1912 to 1975.
Grégoire Marcellin, 47 years old, employed as a chafing cook at Chocolats Célui, volunteers to replace the soldier Vatré, who cannot overcome fears overwhelming him before, during, and after assuming his post.
Placed in the Sainte-Anne Psychiatric Center. Medical certificate from Dr. Replatet.
Delirious syndrome of persecution, hallucinations, says he is attacked night and day by the Mesopotamian funereal pieces in the Musée du Louvre.
1926, Euzèbe Dupommard, relieved of duty. Claims to feel hostile presences during his duty hours.
Cohorts of little sculptures were plotting to poison his brain.
1957 - Firmin Marmandier, summary suspension after 3 weeks in service. Can no longer bear "the mockery and insults towards him from the Rembrandt pieces," had to interrupt his rounds among the Italian paintings because of the terrifying shouts seeking to drive him from the museum.
1963 - Herbert Manfredmann. Claims that the varnish on the paintings is diffusing a fatal gas meant to eliminate him.
1972 - Édouard Paneck. Maintains that, every night, the museum seeks to devour him.
1974 - Fu Zhi Ha, deaf, art history student. Shows a psychotic state with hallucinations relative to his night watch. Delirious paralogism. Esoteric obsessions. Veneration for musical instruments which, in his words, "keep the museum under perfusion."

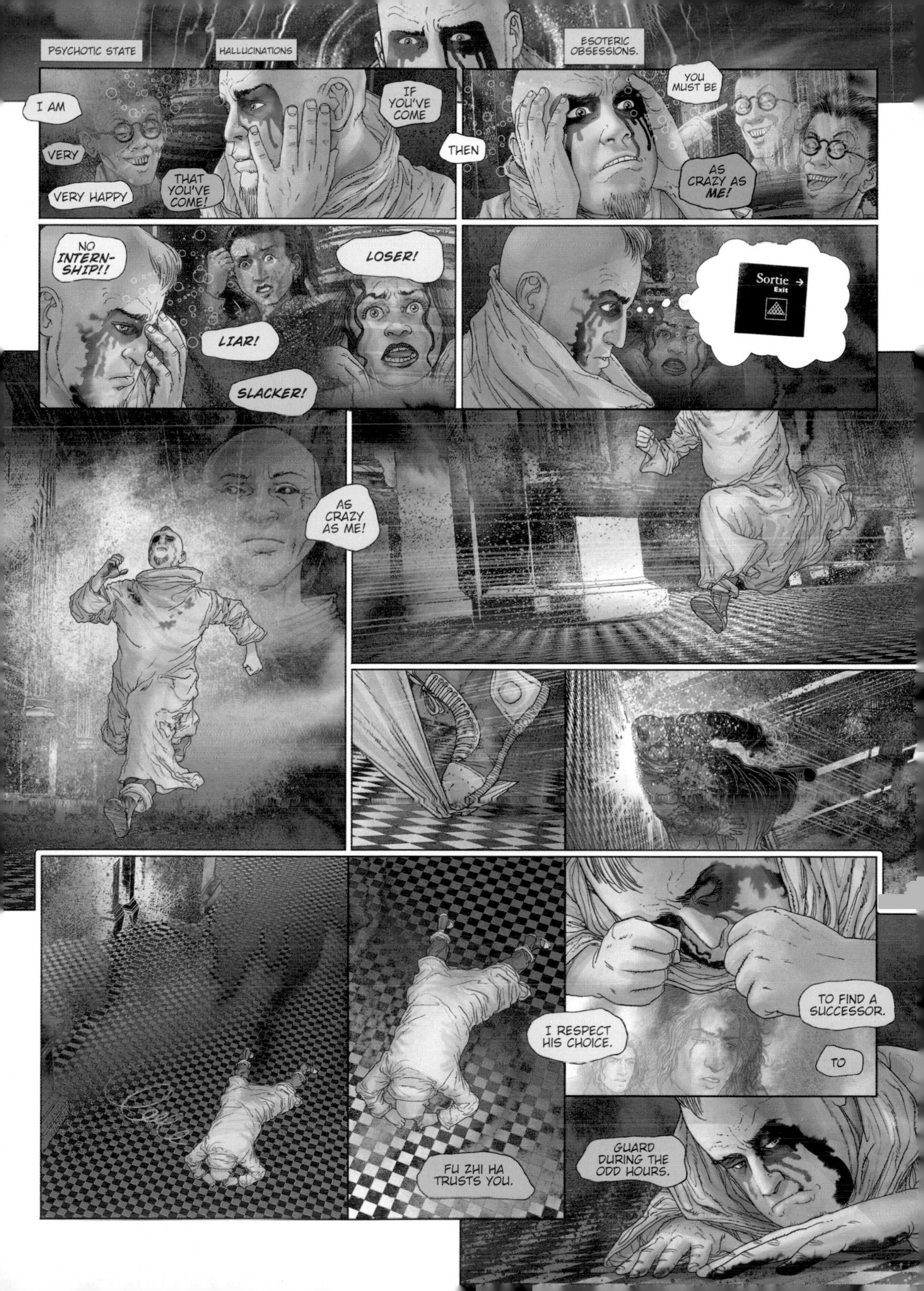

PSYCHOTIC STATE
HALLUCINATIONS
ESOTERIC OBSESSIONS.
I AM
VERY
VERY HAPPY
THAT YOU'VE COME!
IF YOU'VE COME
THEN
YOU MUST BE
AS CRAZY AS ME!
NO INTERN-SHIP!!
LOSER!
LIAR!
SLACKER!
Sortie
Exit
AS CRAZY AS ME!
TO FIND A SUCCESSOR.
I RESPECT HIS CHOICE.
TO
GUARD DURING THE ODD HOURS.
FU ZHI HA TRUSTS YOU.

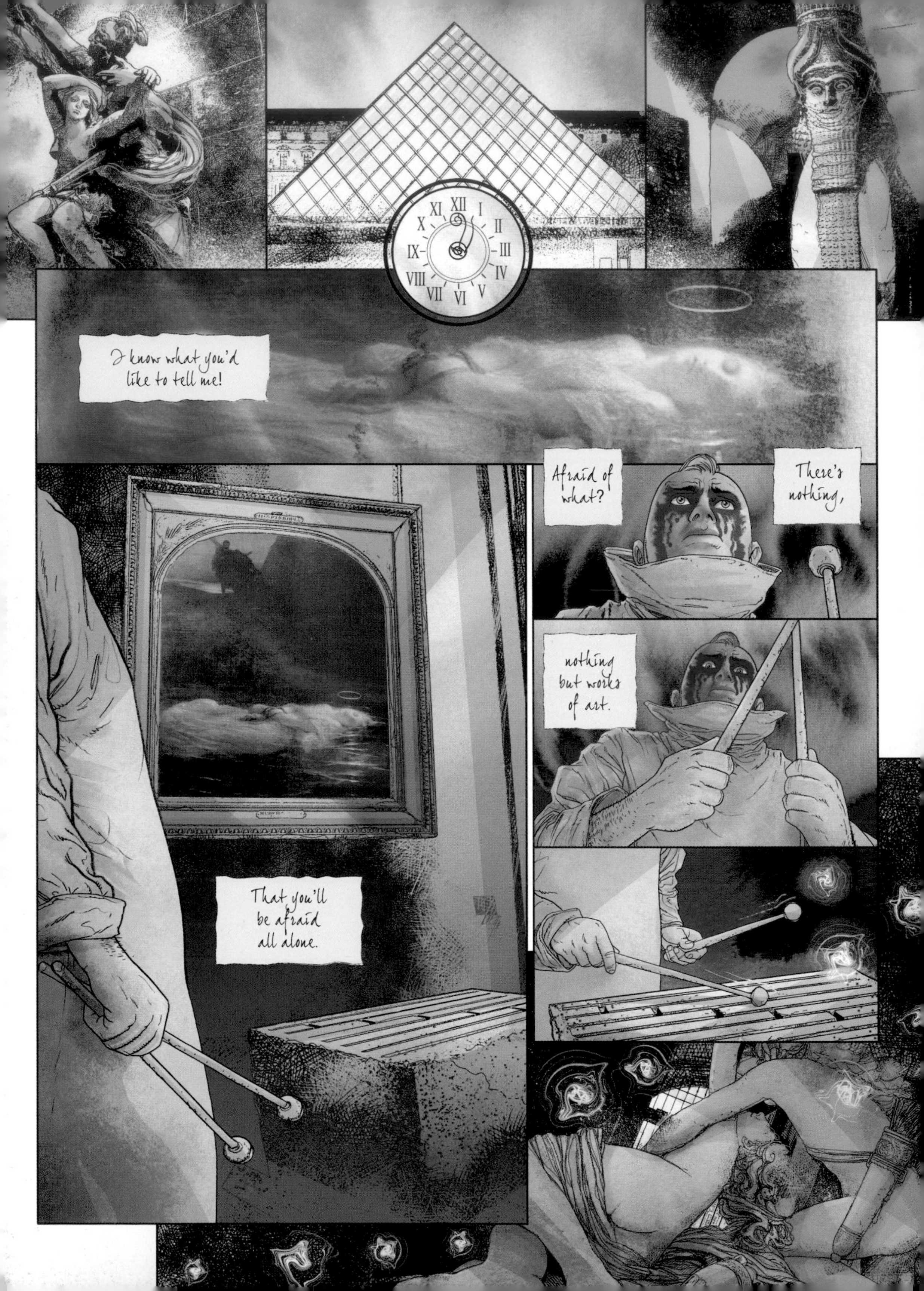
XII I II III IV V VI VII VIII IX X XI
I know what you'd like to tell me!
That you'll be afraid all alone.
Afraid of what?
There's nothing,
nothing but works of art.

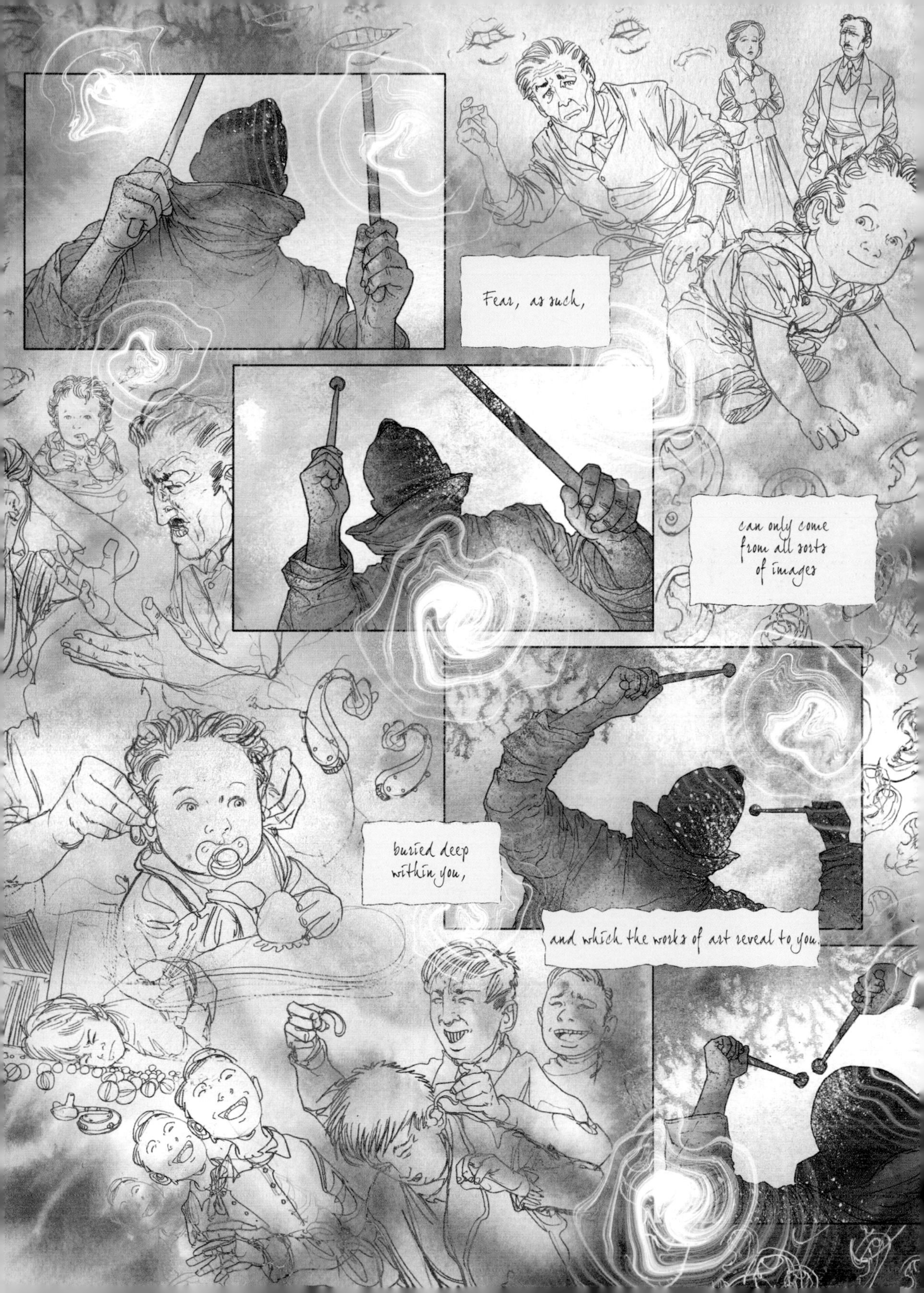
Fear, as such,
can only come from all sorts of images
buried deep within you,
and which the works of art reveal to you.

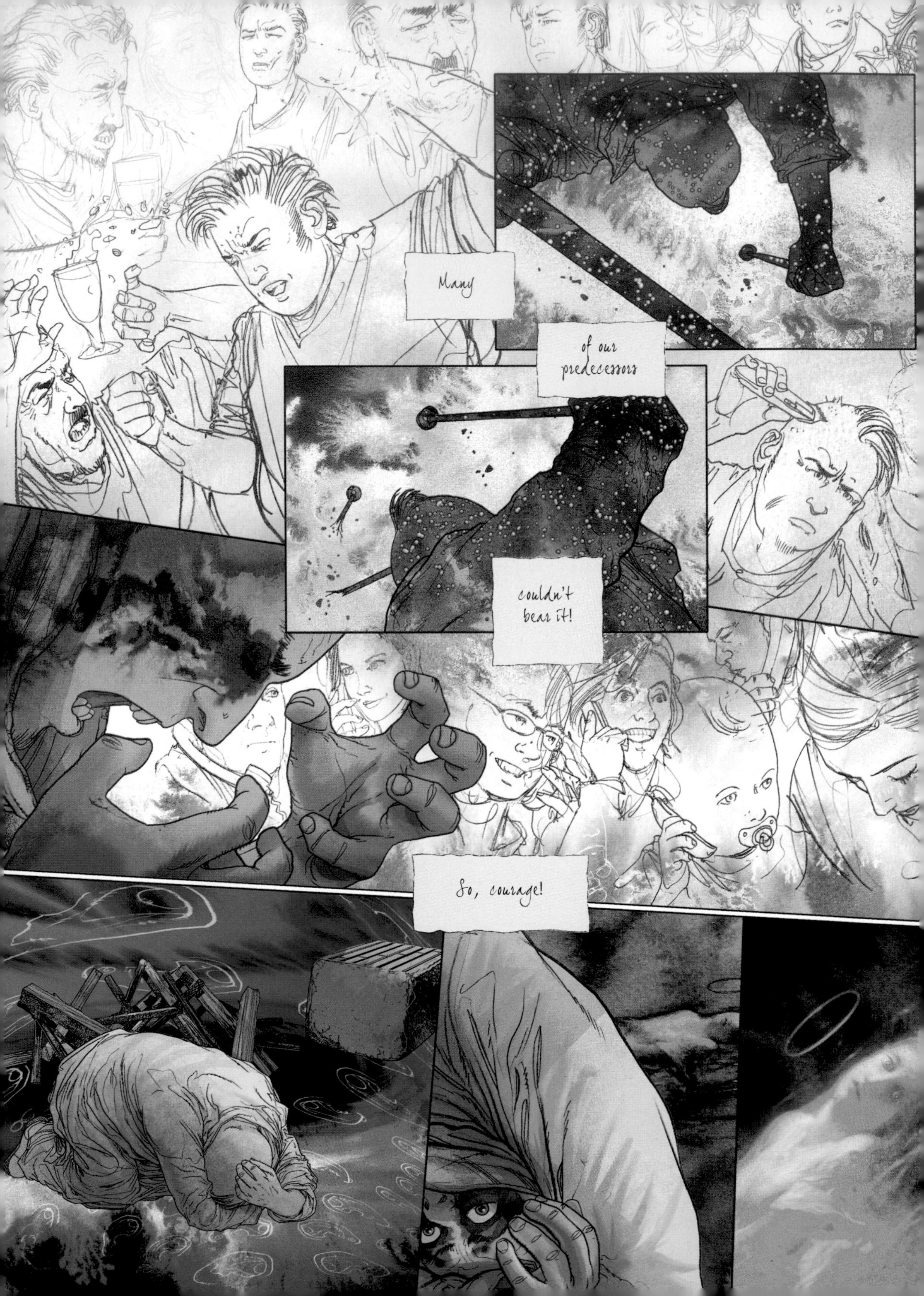
Many
of our predecessors
couldn't bear it!
So, courage!

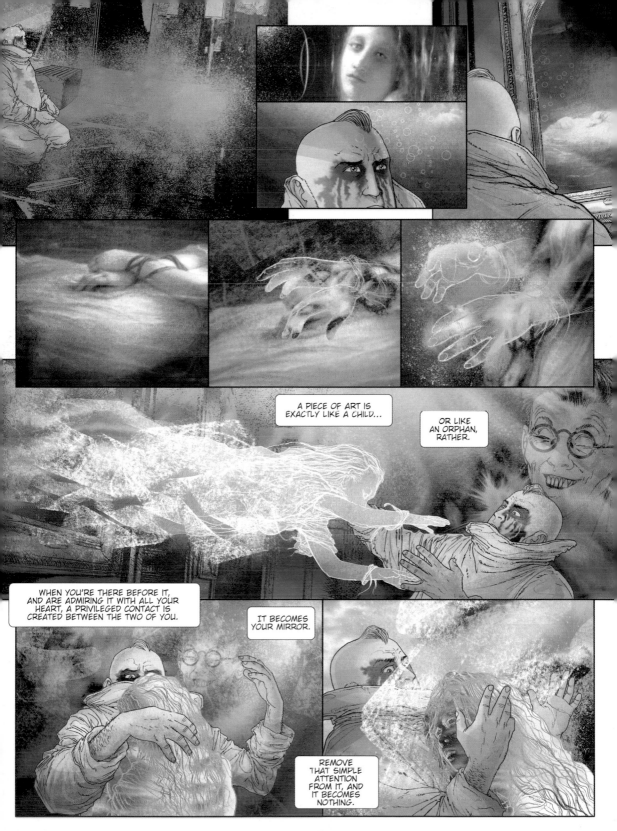

A PIECE OF ART IS EXACTLY LIKE A CHILD...

OR LIKE AN ORPHAN, RATHER.

WHEN YOU'RE THERE BEFORE IT, AND ARE ADMIRING IT WITH ALL YOUR HEART, A PRIVILEGED CONTACT IS CREATED BETWEEN THE TWO OF YOU.

IT BECOMES YOUR MIRROR.

REMOVE THAT SIMPLE ATTENTION FROM IT, AND IT BECOMES NOTHING.

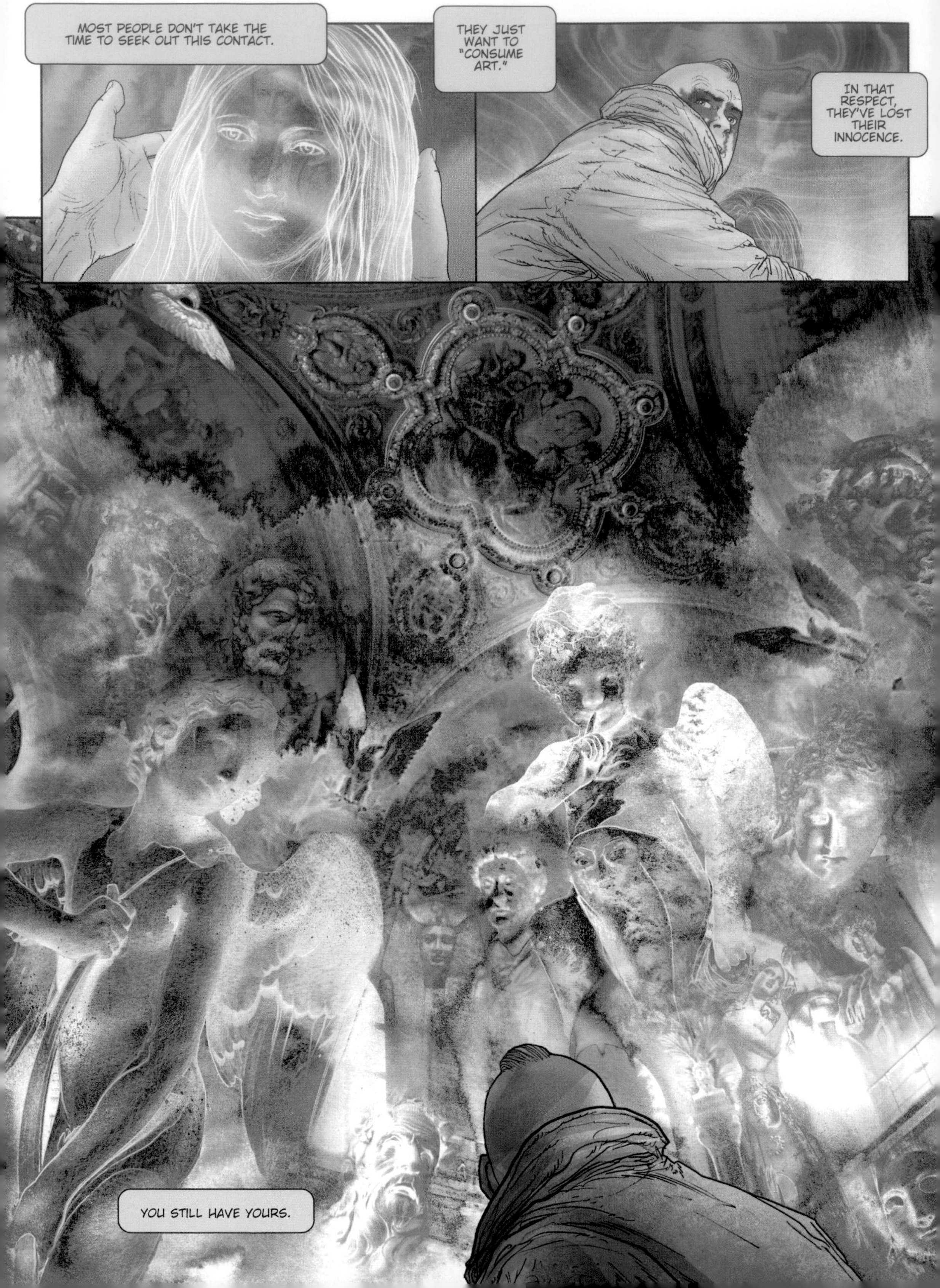
MOST PEOPLE DON'T TAKE THE TIME TO SEEK OUT THIS CONTACT.
THEY JUST WANT TO "CONSUME ART."
IN THAT RESPECT, THEY'VE LOST THEIR INNOCENCE.
YOU STILL HAVE YOURS.

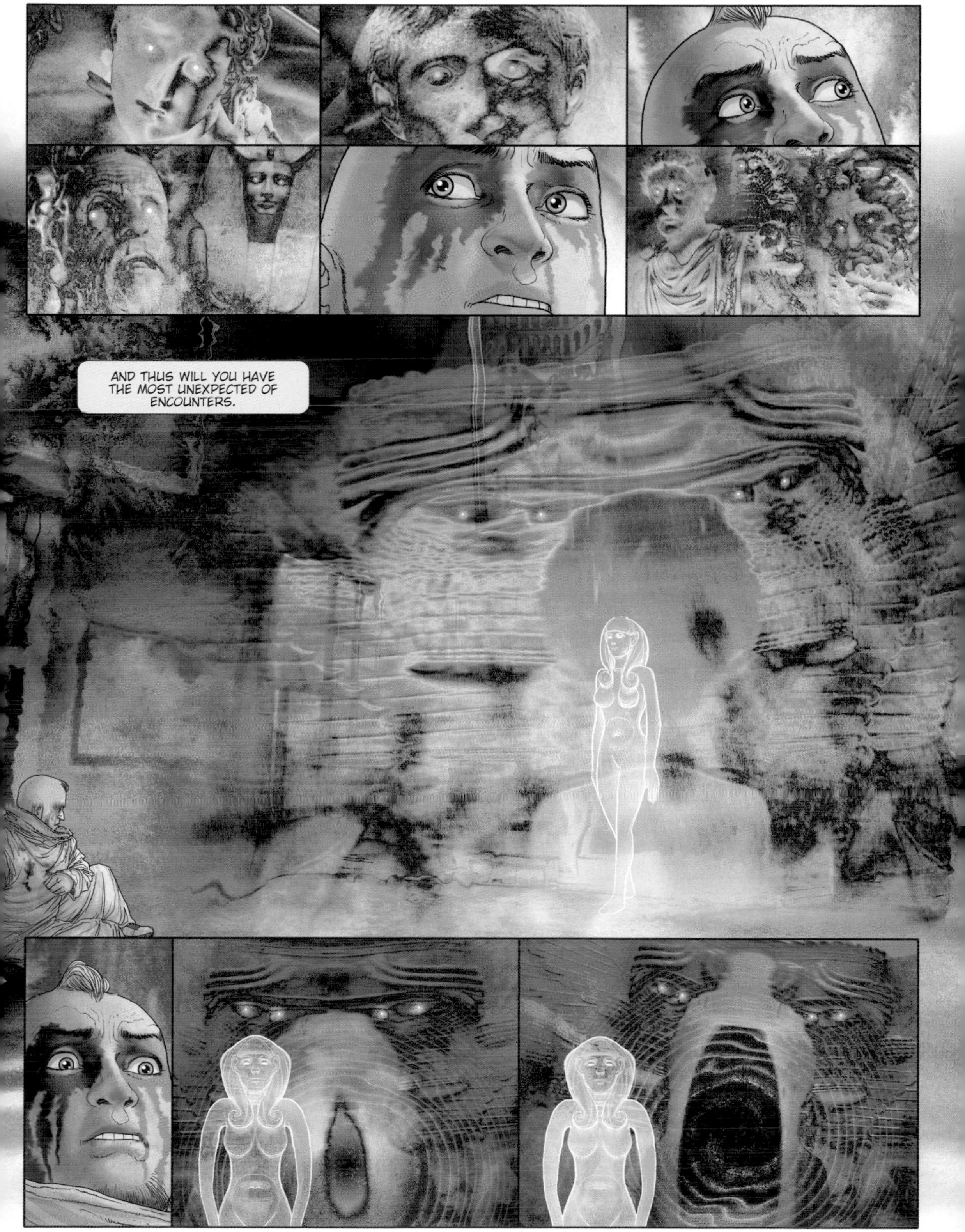
AND THUS WILL YOU HAVE THE MOST UNEXPECTED OF ENCOUNTERS.

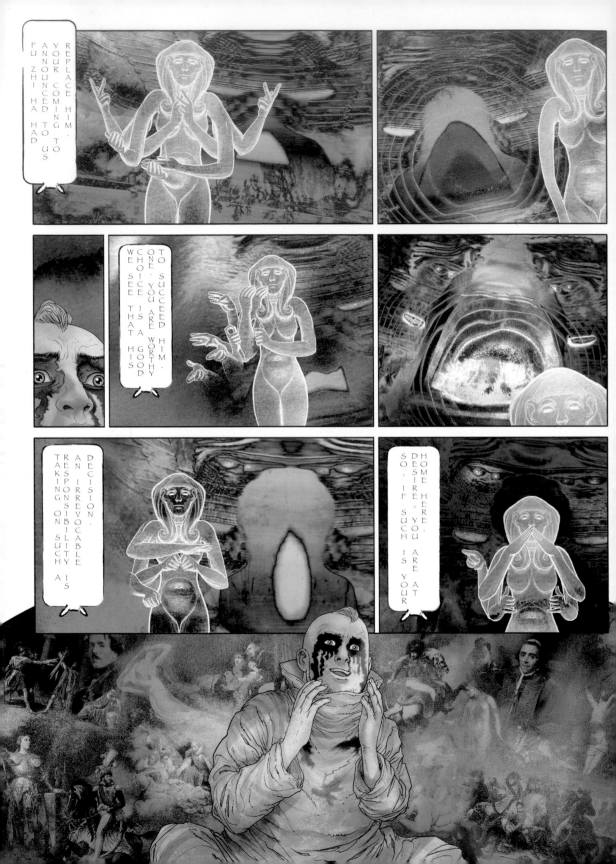

FU ZHI HAD FANTASIZED ANNOUNCED TO US YOUR COMING TO REPLACE HIM.

WE SEE THAT HIS CHOICE IS A GOOD ONE. YOU ARE WORTHY TO SUCCEED HIM.

TAKING ON SUCH A RESPONSIBILITY IS AN IRREVOCABLE DECISION.

SO, IF SUCH IS YOUR DESIRE, YOU ARE AT HOME HERE.

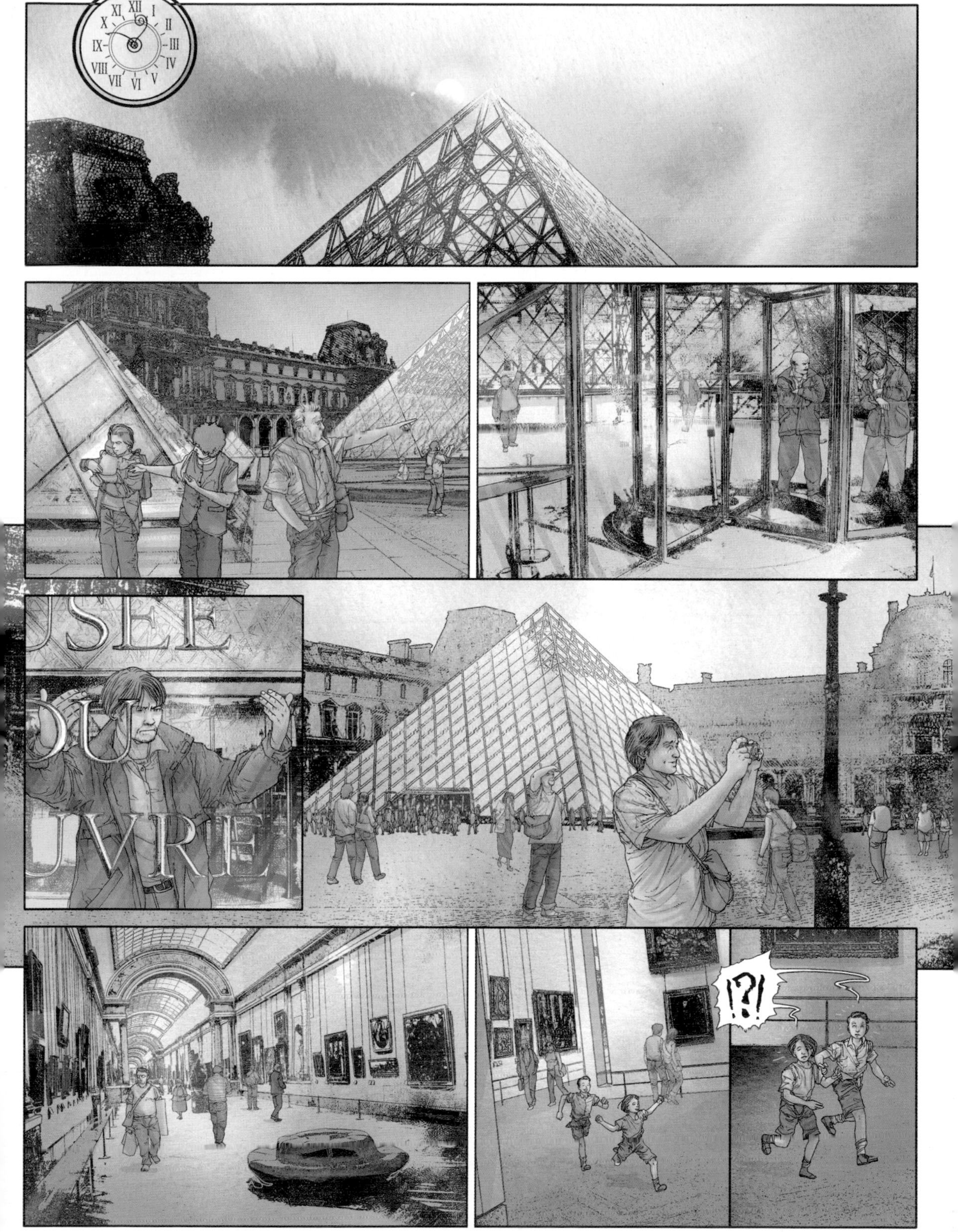
USEE
DU
UVRE
!?!

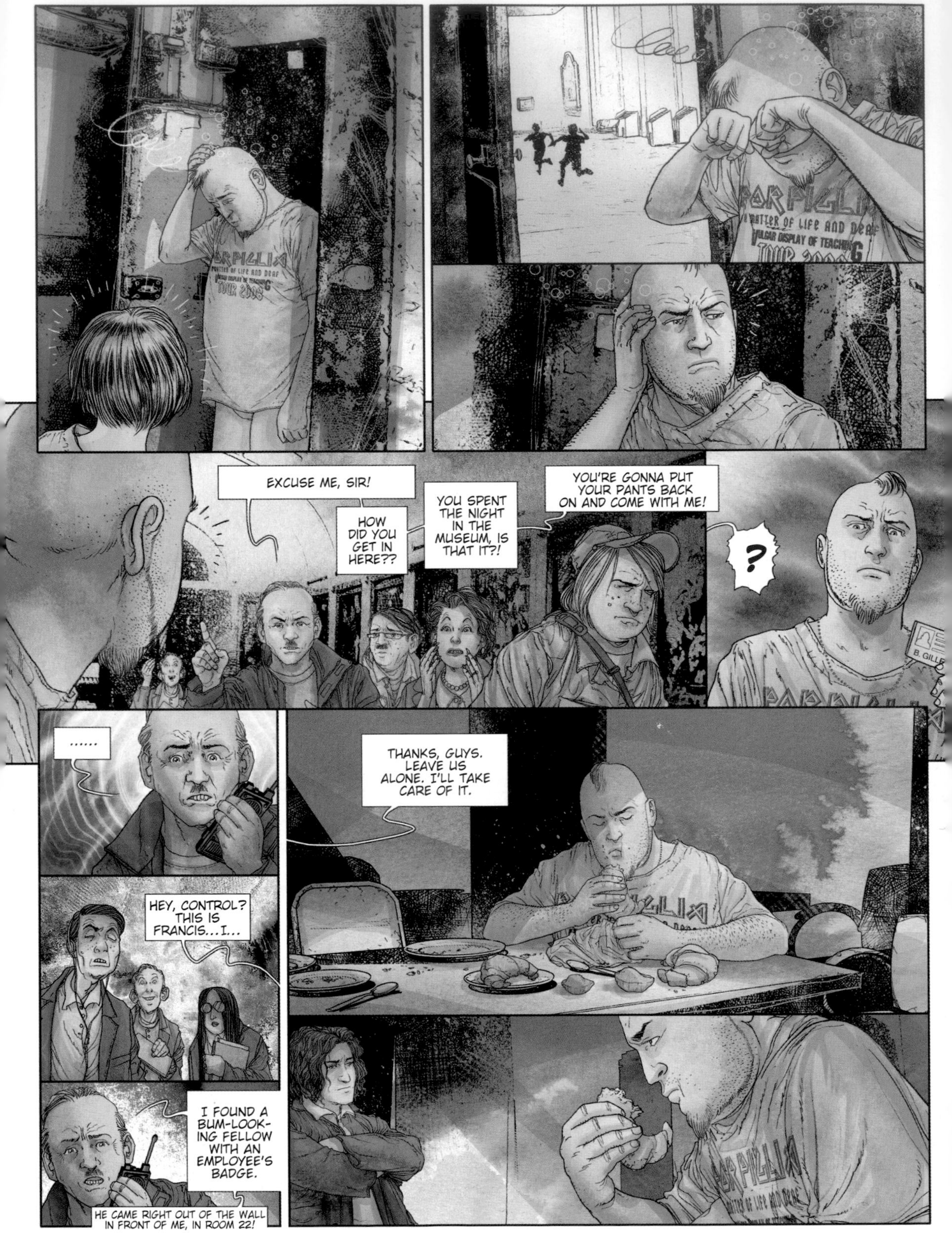

EXCUSE ME, SIR!
HOW DID YOU GET IN HERE??
YOU SPENT THE NIGHT IN THE MUSEUM, IS THAT IT?!
YOU'RE GONNA PUT YOUR PANTS BACK ON AND COME WITH ME!
?
......
HEY, CONTROL? THIS IS FRANCIS... I...
I FOUND A BUM-LOOKING FELLOW WITH AN EMPLOYEE'S BADGE.
HE CAME RIGHT OUT OF THE WALL IN FRONT OF ME, IN ROOM 22!
THANKS, GUYS. LEAVE US ALONE. I'LL TAKE CARE OF IT.

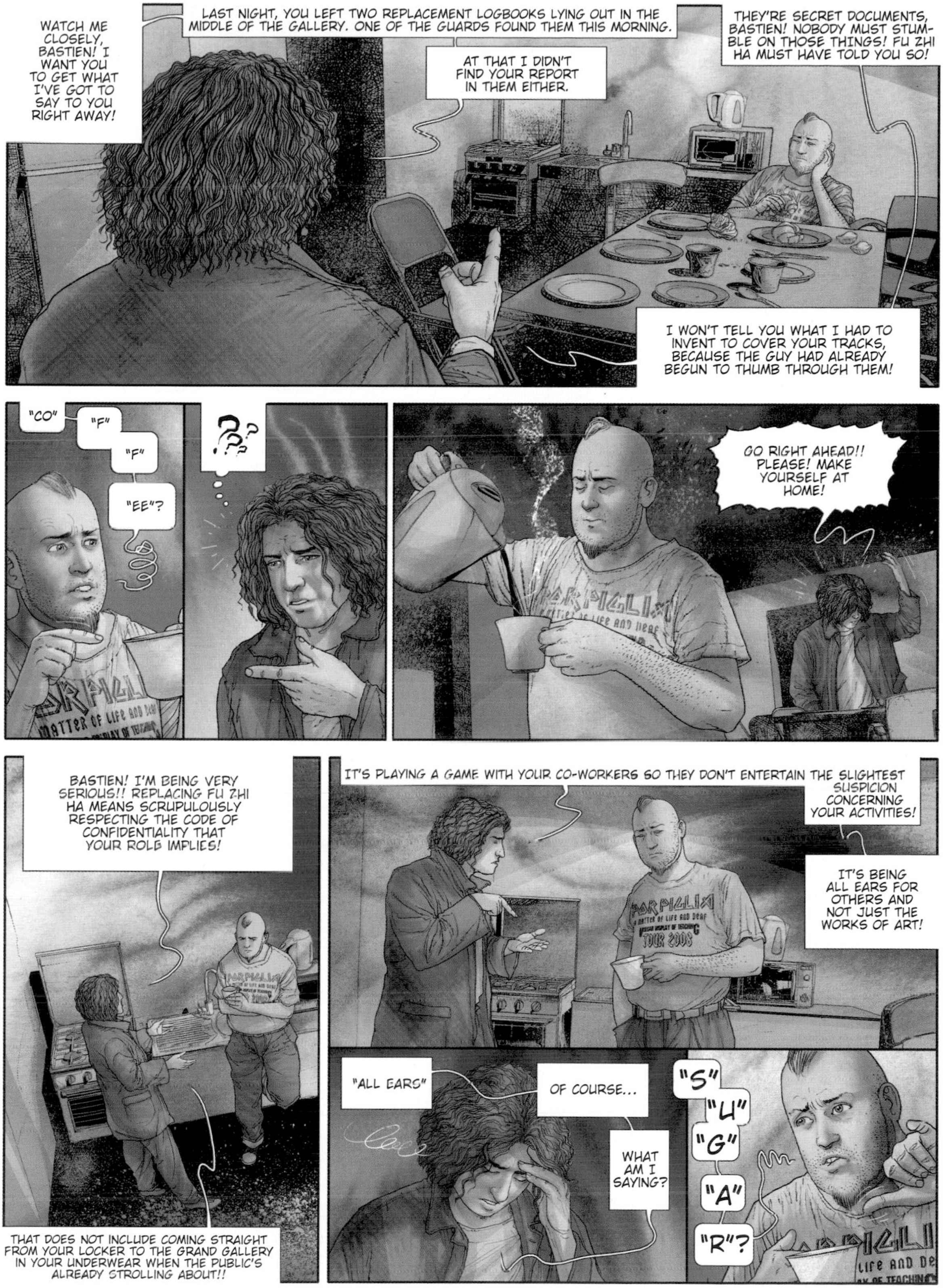

WATCH ME CLOSELY, BASTIEN! I WANT YOU TO GET WHAT I'VE GOT TO SAY TO YOU RIGHT AWAY!
LAST NIGHT, YOU LEFT TWO REPLACEMENT LOGBOOKS LYING OUT IN THE MIDDLE OF THE GALLERY. ONE OF THE GUARDS FOUND THEM THIS MORNING.
AT THAT I DIDN'T FIND YOUR REPORT IN THEM EITHER.
THEY'RE SECRET DOCUMENTS, BASTIEN! NOBODY MUST STUMBLE ON THOSE THINGS! FU ZHI HA MUST HAVE TOLD YOU SO!
I WON'T TELL YOU WHAT I HAD TO INVENT TO COVER YOUR TRACKS, BECAUSE THE GUY HAD ALREADY BEGUN TO THUMB THROUGH THEM!
"CO"
"F"
"F"
"EE"?
???
GO RIGHT AHEAD!! PLEASE! MAKE YOURSELF AT HOME!
BASTIEN! I'M BEING VERY SERIOUS!! REPLACING FU ZHI HA MEANS SCRUPULOUSLY RESPECTING THE CODE OF CONFIDENTIALITY THAT YOUR ROLE IMPLIES!
THAT DOES NOT INCLUDE COMING STRAIGHT FROM YOUR LOCKER TO THE GRAND GALLERY IN YOUR UNDERWEAR WHEN THE PUBLIC'S ALREADY STROLLING ABOUT!!
IT'S PLAYING A GAME WITH YOUR CO-WORKERS SO THEY DON'T ENTERTAIN THE SLIGHTEST SUSPICION CONCERNING YOUR ACTIVITIES!
IT'S BEING ALL EARS FOR OTHERS AND NOT JUST THE WORKS OF ART!
"ALL EARS"
OF COURSE...
WHAT AM I SAYING?
"S"
"U"
"G"
"A"
"R"?

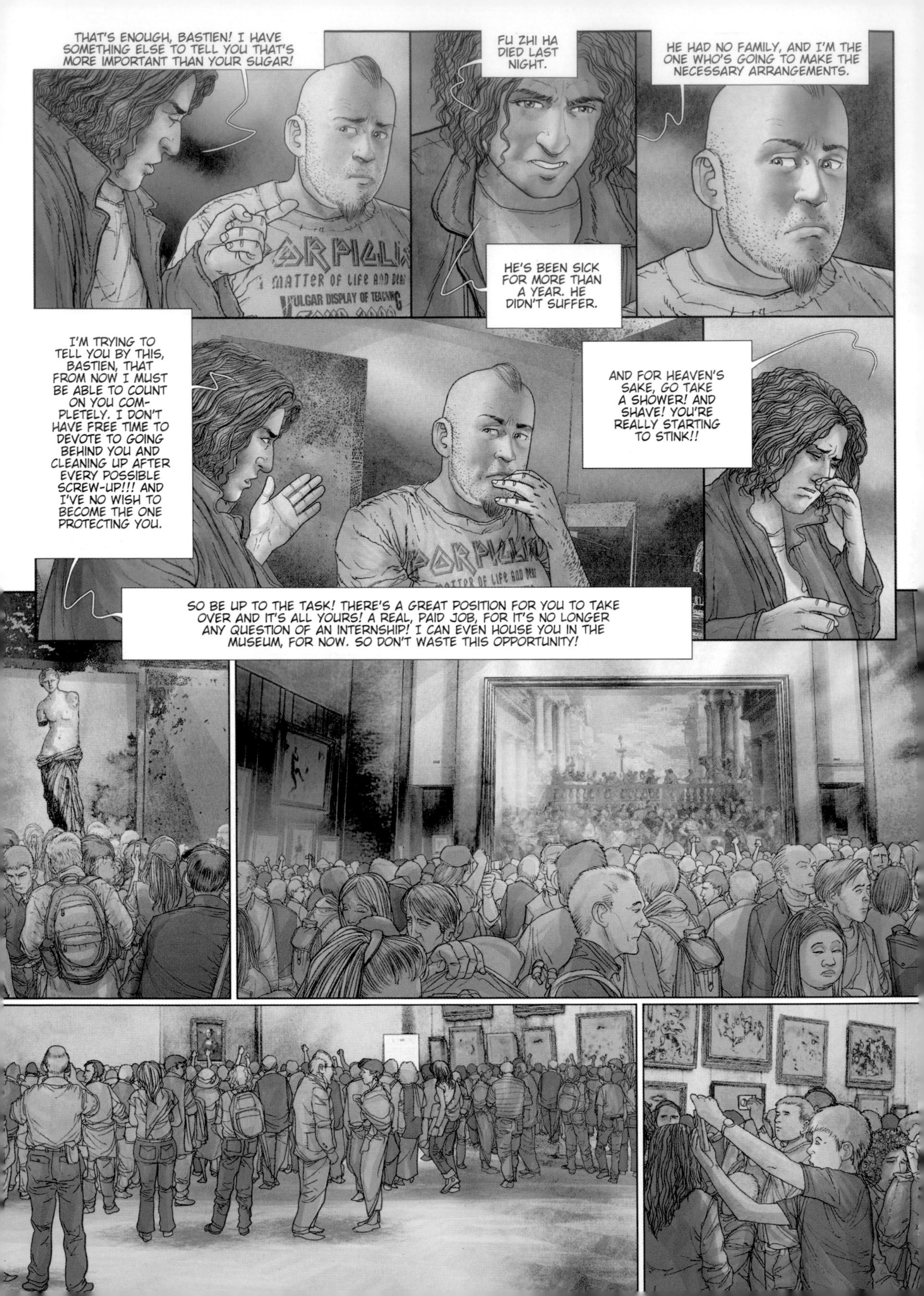
THAT'S ENOUGH, BASTIEN! I HAVE SOMETHING ELSE TO TELL YOU THAT'S MORE IMPORTANT THAN YOUR SUGAR!
FU ZHI HA DIED LAST NIGHT.
HE'S BEEN SICK FOR MORE THAN A YEAR. HE DIDN'T SUFFER.
HE HAD NO FAMILY, AND I'M THE ONE WHO'S GOING TO MAKE THE NECESSARY ARRANGEMENTS.
I'M TRYING TO TELL YOU BY THIS, BASTIEN, THAT FROM NOW I MUST BE ABLE TO COUNT ON YOU COMPLETELY. I DON'T HAVE FREE TIME TO DEVOTE TO GOING BEHIND YOU AND CLEANING UP AFTER EVERY POSSIBLE SCREW-UP!!! AND I'VE NO WISH TO BECOME THE ONE PROTECTING YOU.
AND FOR HEAVEN'S SAKE, GO TAKE A SHOWER! AND SHAVE! YOU'RE REALLY STARTING TO STINK!!
SO BE UP TO THE TASK! THERE'S A GREAT POSITION FOR YOU TO TAKE OVER AND IT'S ALL YOURS! A REAL, PAID JOB, FOR IT'S NO LONGER ANY QUESTION OF AN INTERNSHIP! I CAN EVEN HOUSE YOU IN THE MUSEUM, FOR NOW. SO DON'T WASTE THIS OPPORTUNITY!

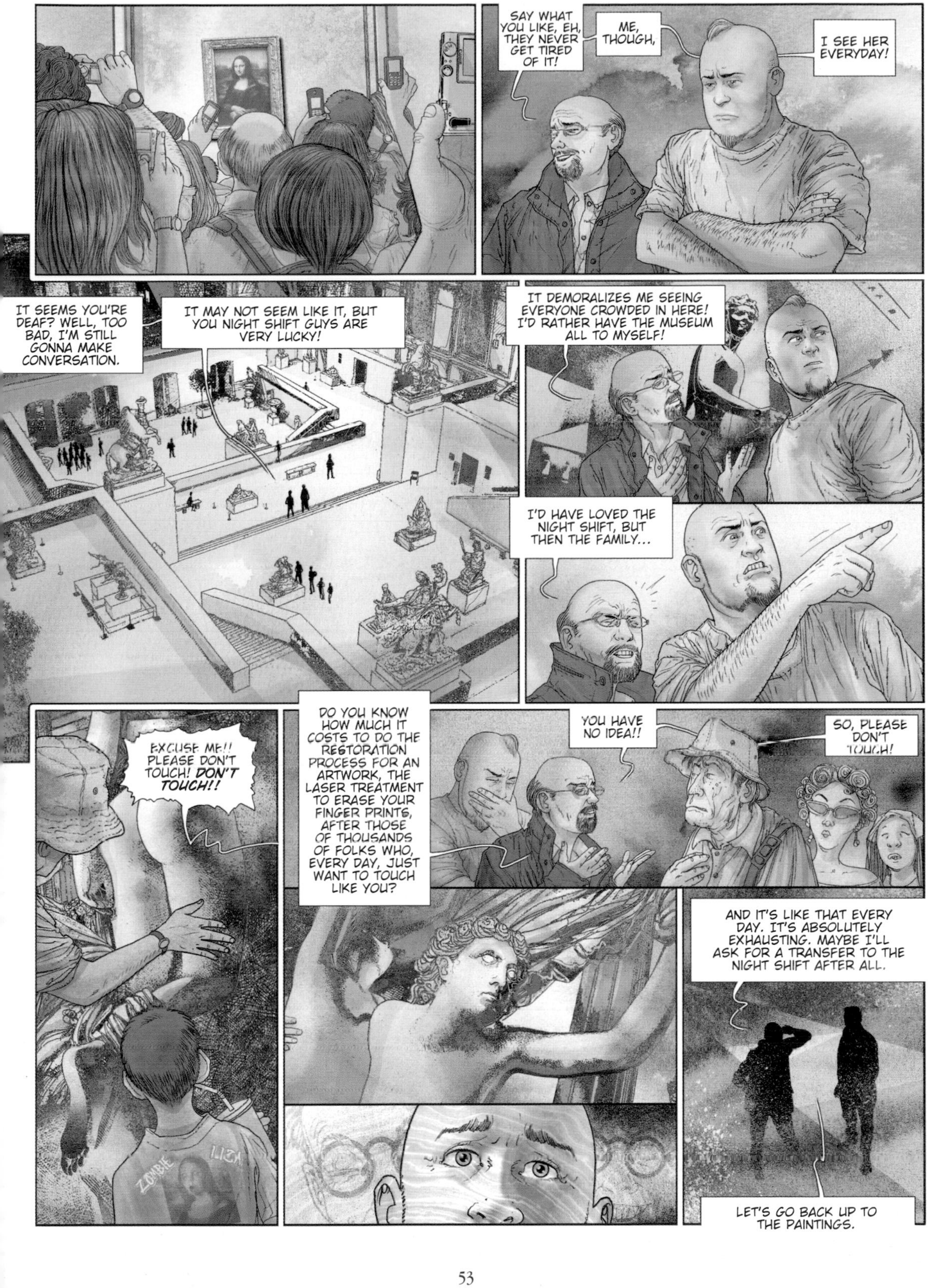
SAY WHAT YOU LIKE, EH, THEY NEVER GET TIRED OF IT!
ME, THOUGH,
I SEE HER EVERYDAY!
IT SEEMS YOU'RE DEAF? WELL, TOO BAD, I'M STILL GONNA MAKE CONVERSATION.
IT MAY NOT SEEM LIKE IT, BUT YOU NIGHT SHIFT GUYS ARE VERY LUCKY!
IT DEMORALIZES ME SEEING EVERYONE CROWDED IN HERE! I'D RATHER HAVE THE MUSEUM ALL TO MYSELF!
I'D HAVE LOVED THE NIGHT SHIFT, BUT THEN THE FAMILY...
EXCUSE ME!! PLEASE DON'T TOUCH! DON'T TOUCH!!
DO YOU KNOW HOW MUCH IT COSTS TO DO THE RESTORATION PROCESS FOR AN ARTWORK, THE LASER TREATMENT TO ERASE YOUR FINGER PRINTS, AFTER THOSE OF THOUSANDS OF FOLKS WHO, EVERY DAY, JUST WANT TO TOUCH LIKE YOU?
YOU HAVE NO IDEA!!
SO, PLEASE DON'T TOUCH!
ZOMBIE LISA
AND IT'S LIKE THAT EVERY DAY. IT'S ABSOLUTELY EXHAUSTING. MAYBE I'LL ASK FOR A TRANSFER TO THE NIGHT SHIFT AFTER ALL.
LET'S GO BACK UP TO THE PAINTINGS.

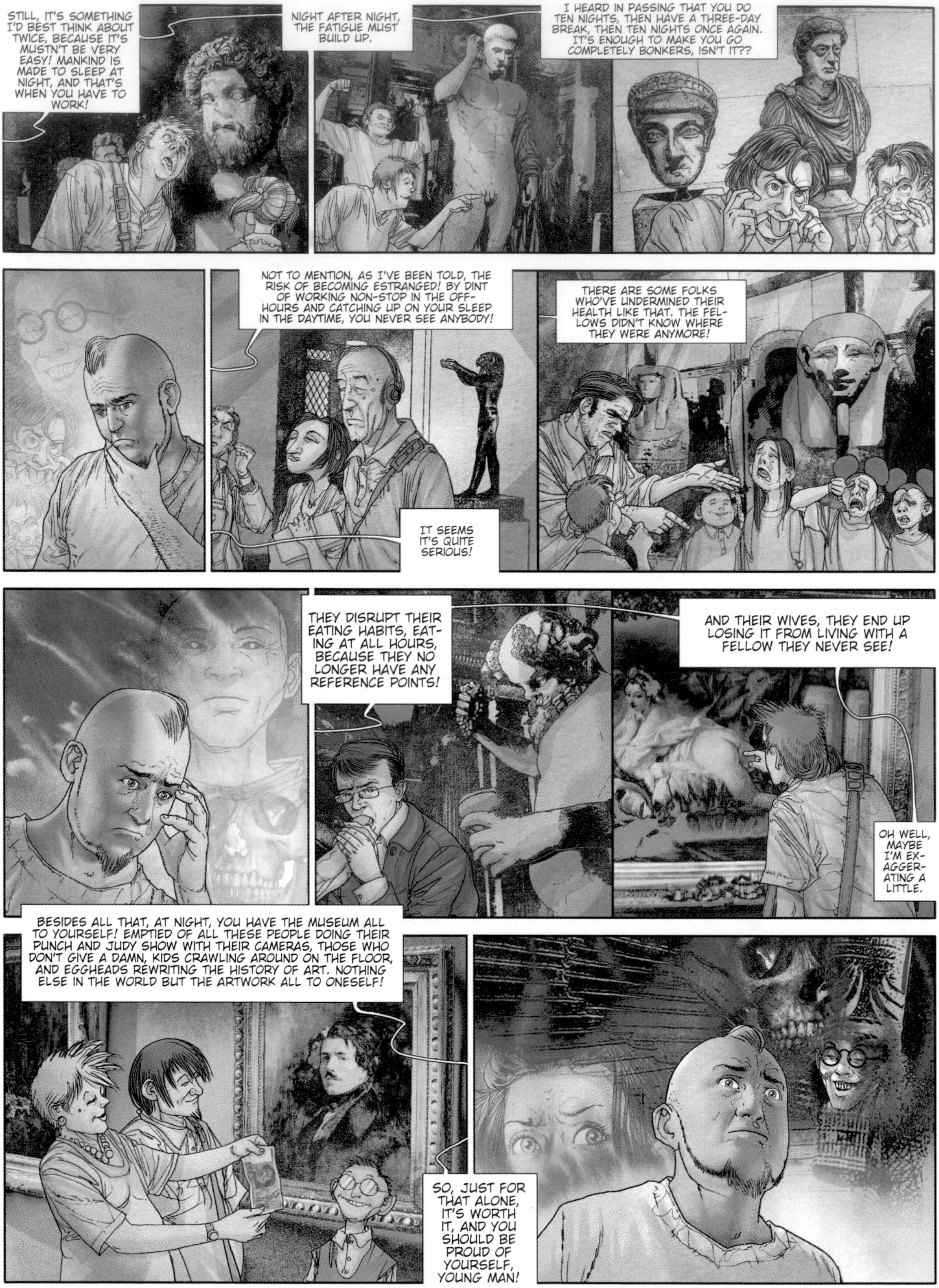
STILL, IT'S SOMETHING I'D BEST THINK ABOUT TWICE, BECAUSE IT'S MUSTN'T BE VERY EASY! MANKIND IS MADE TO SLEEP AT NIGHT, AND THAT'S WHEN YOU HAVE TO WORK!
NIGHT AFTER NIGHT, THE FATIGUE MUST BUILD UP.
I HEARD IN PASSING THAT YOU DO TEN NIGHTS, THEN HAVE A THREE-DAY BREAK, THEN TEN NIGHTS ONCE AGAIN. IT'S ENOUGH TO MAKE YOU GO COMPLETELY BONKERS, ISN'T IT??
NOT TO MENTION, AS I'VE BEEN TOLD, THE RISK OF BECOMING ESTRANGED! BY DINT OF WORKING NON-STOP IN THE OFF-HOURS AND CATCHING UP ON YOUR SLEEP IN THE DAYTIME, YOU NEVER SEE ANYBODY!
IT SEEMS IT'S QUITE SERIOUS!
THERE ARE SOME FOLKS WHO'VE UNDERMINED THEIR HEALTH LIKE THAT. THE FEL-LOWS DIDN'T KNOW WHERE THEY WERE ANYMORE!
THEY DISRUPT THEIR EATING HABITS, EAT-ING AT ALL HOURS, BECAUSE THEY NO LONGER HAVE ANY REFERENCE POINTS!
AND THEIR WIVES, THEY END UP LOSING IT FROM LIVING WITH A FELLOW THEY NEVER SEE!
OH WELL, MAYBE I'M EX-AGGER-ATING A LITTLE.
BESIDES ALL THAT, AT NIGHT, YOU HAVE THE MUSEUM ALL TO YOURSELF! EMPTIED OF ALL THESE PEOPLE DOING THEIR PUNCH AND JUDY SHOW WITH THEIR CAMERAS, THOSE WHO DON'T GIVE A DAMN, KIDS CRAWLING AROUND ON THE FLOOR, AND EGGHEADS REWRITING THE HISTORY OF ART. NOTHING ELSE IN THE WORLD BUT THE ARTWORK ALL TO ONESELF!
SO, JUST FOR THAT ALONE, IT'S WORTH IT, AND YOU SHOULD BE PROUD OF YOURSELF, YOUNG MAN!

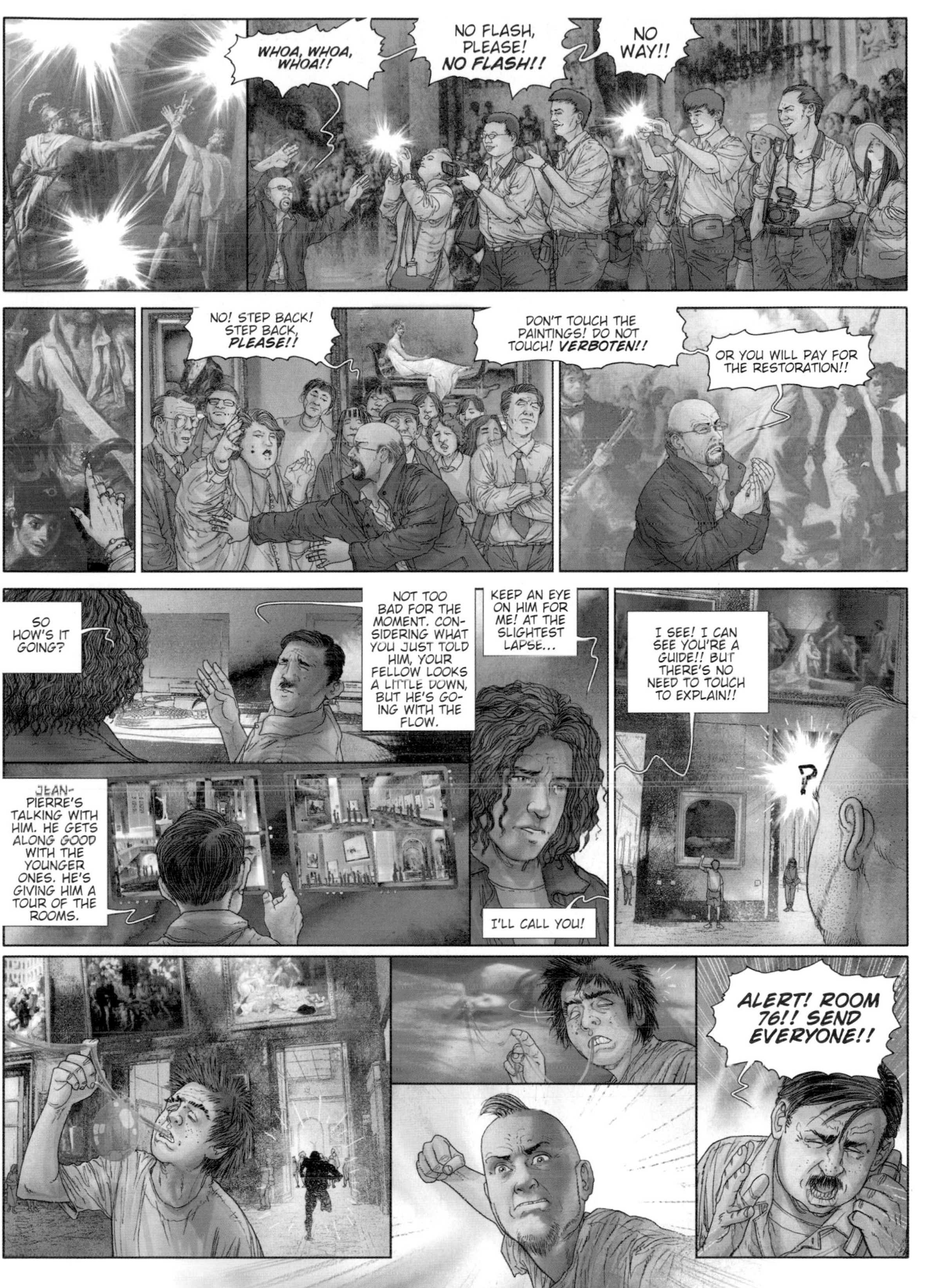
WHOA, WHOA, WHOA!!
NO FLASH, PLEASE! NO FLASH!!
NO WAY!!
NO! STEP BACK! STEP BACK, PLEASE!!
DON'T TOUCH THE PAINTINGS! DO NOT TOUCH! VERBOTEN!!
OR YOU WILL PAY FOR THE RESTORATION!!
SO HOW'S IT GOING?
NOT TOO BAD FOR THE MOMENT. CONSIDERING WHAT YOU JUST TOLD HIM, YOUR FELLOW LOOKS A LITTLE DOWN, BUT HE'S GOING WITH THE FLOW.
JEAN-PIERRE'S TALKING WITH HIM. HE GETS ALONG GOOD WITH THE YOUNGER ONES. HE'S GIVING HIM A TOUR OF THE ROOMS.
KEEP AN EYE ON HIM FOR ME! AT THE SLIGHTEST LAPSE...
I'LL CALL YOU!
I SEE! I CAN SEE YOU'RE A GUIDE!! BUT THERE'S NO NEED TO TOUCH TO EXPLAIN!!
?
ALERT! ROOM 76!! SEND EVERYONE!!

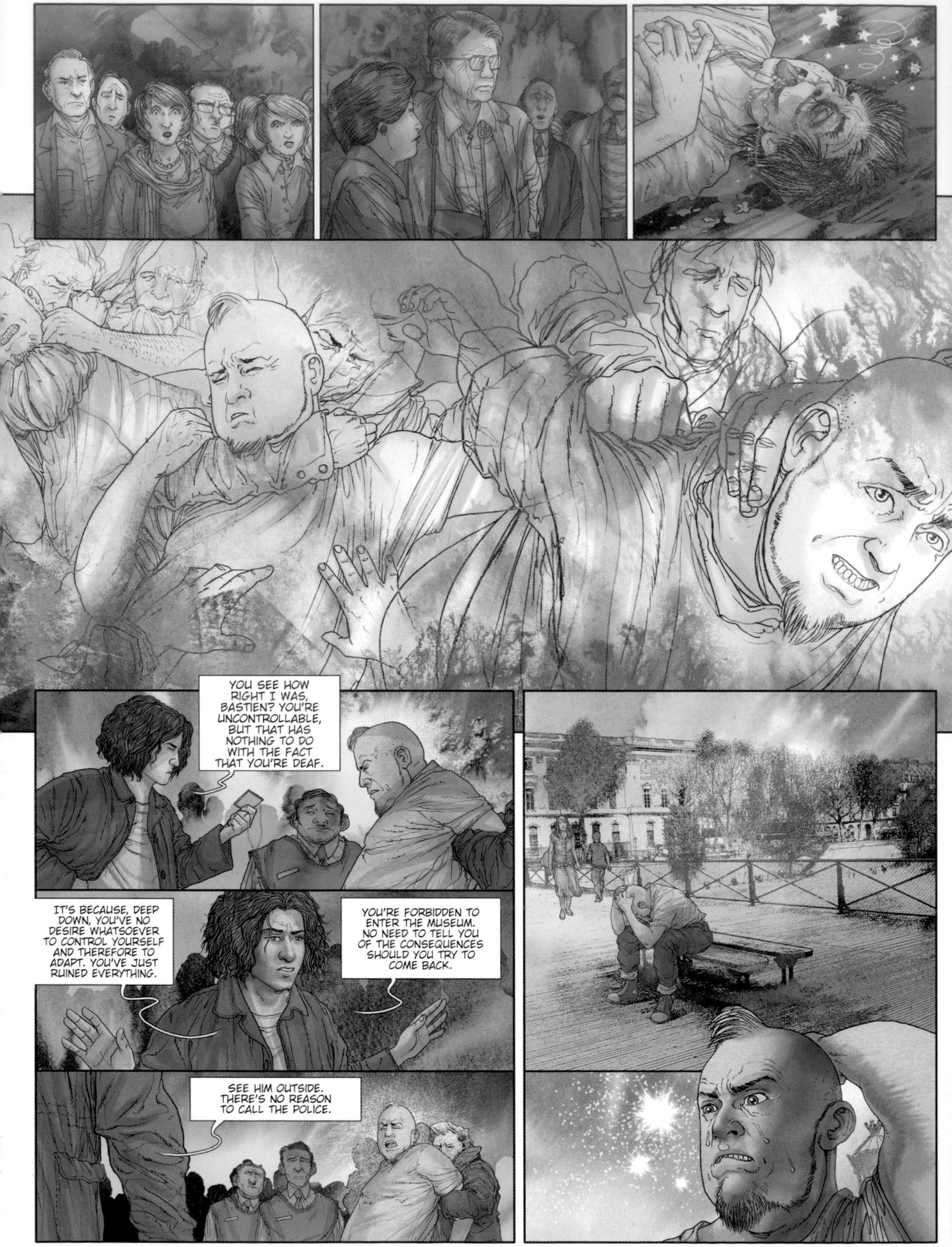
YOU SEE HOW RIGHT I WAS, BASTIEN? YOU'RE UNCONTROLLABLE, BUT THAT HAS NOTHING TO DO WITH THE FACT THAT YOU'RE DEAF.
IT'S BECAUSE, DEEP DOWN, YOU'VE NO DESIRE WHATSOEVER TO CONTROL YOURSELF AND THEREFORE TO ADAPT. YOU'VE JUST RUINED EVERYTHING.
YOU'RE FORBIDDEN TO ENTER THE MUSEUM. NO NEED TO TELL YOU OF THE CONSEQUENCES SHOULD YOU TRY TO COME BACK.
SEE HIM OUTSIDE. THERE'S NO REASON TO CALL THE POLICE.

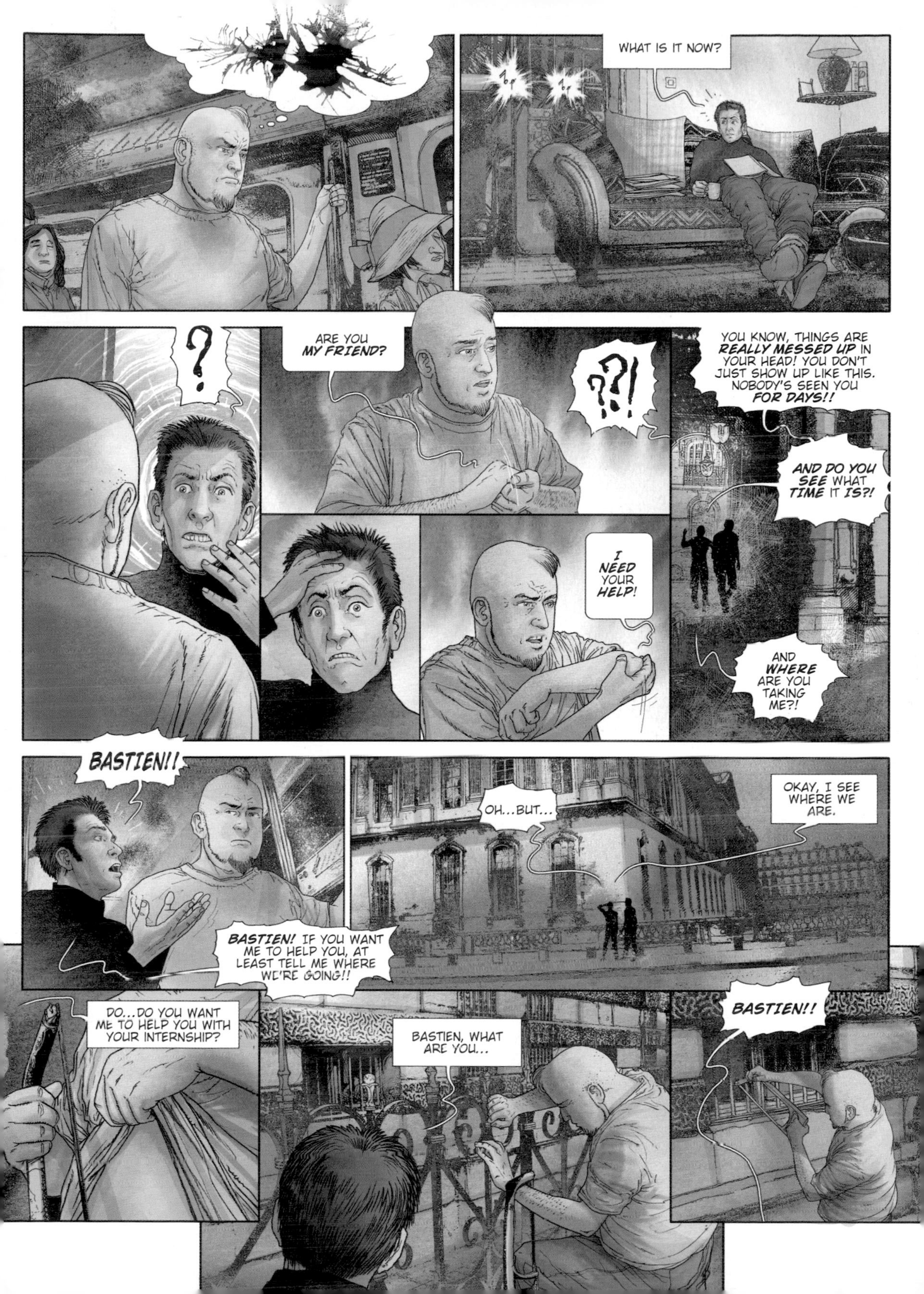
WHAT IS IT NOW?
ARE YOU MY FRIEND?
YOU KNOW, THINGS ARE REALLY MESSED UP IN YOUR HEAD! YOU DON'T JUST SHOW UP LIKE THIS. NOBODY'S SEEN YOU FOR DAYS!!
AND DO YOU SEE WHAT TIME IT IS?!
I NEED YOUR HELP!
AND WHERE ARE YOU TAKING ME?!
BASTIEN!!
OH...BUT...
OKAY, I SEE WHERE WE ARE.
BASTIEN! IF YOU WANT ME TO HELP YOU, AT LEAST TELL ME WHERE WE'RE GOING!!
DO...DO YOU WANT ME TO HELP YOU WITH YOUR INTERNSHIP?
BASTIEN, WHAT ARE YOU...
BASTIEN!!

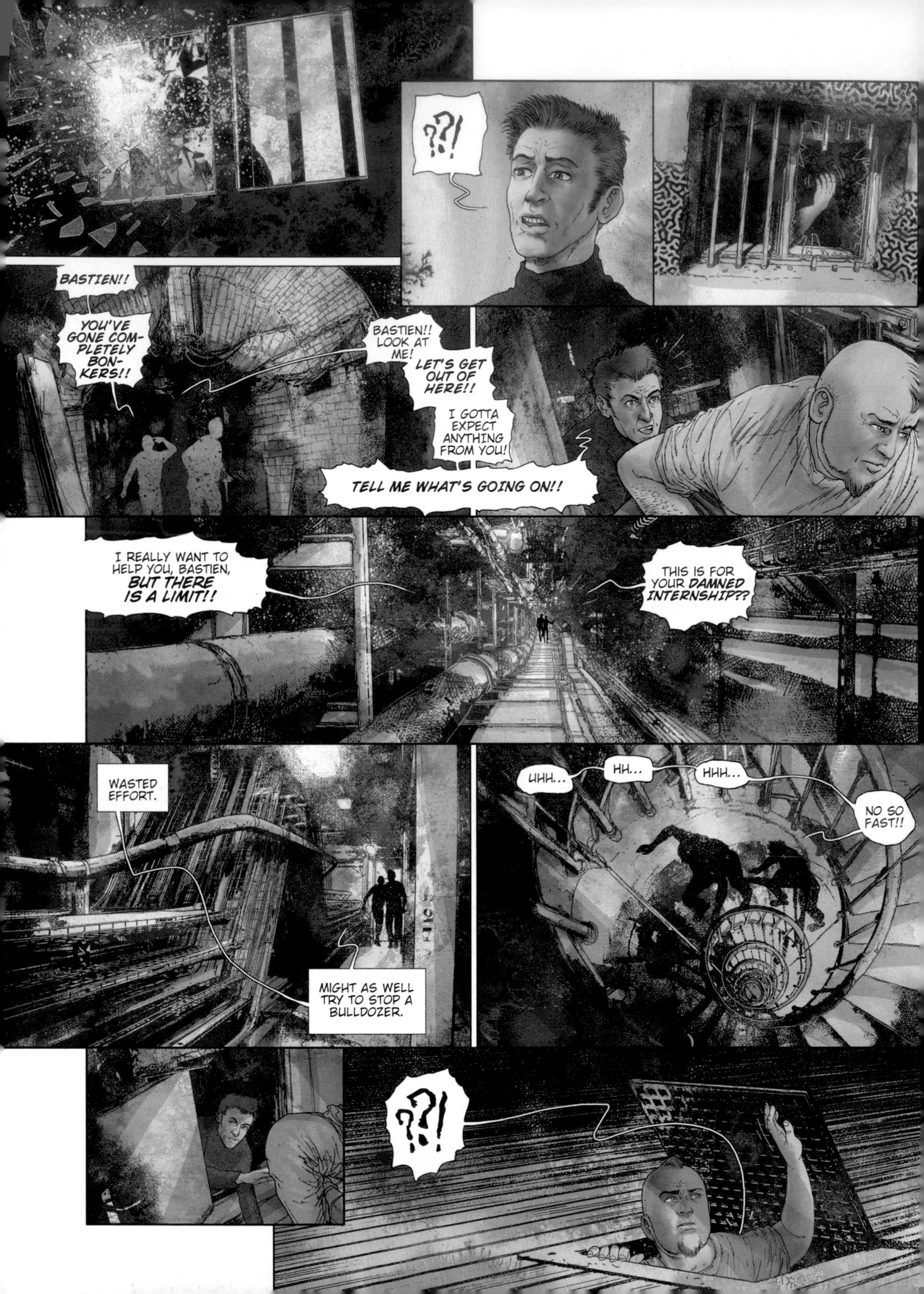
?!?!
BASTIEN!!
YOU'VE GONE COMPLETELY BONKERS!!
BASTIEN!! LOOK AT ME!
LET'S GET OUT OF HERE!!
I GOTTA EXPECT ANYTHING FROM YOU!
TELL ME WHAT'S GOING ON!!
I REALLY WANT TO HELP YOU, BASTIEN, BUT THERE IS A LIMIT!!
THIS IS FOR YOUR DAMNED INTERNSHIP??
WASTED EFFORT.
MIGHT AS WELL TRY TO STOP A BULLDOZER.
UHH...
HH...
HHH...
NO SO FAST!!
?!?!

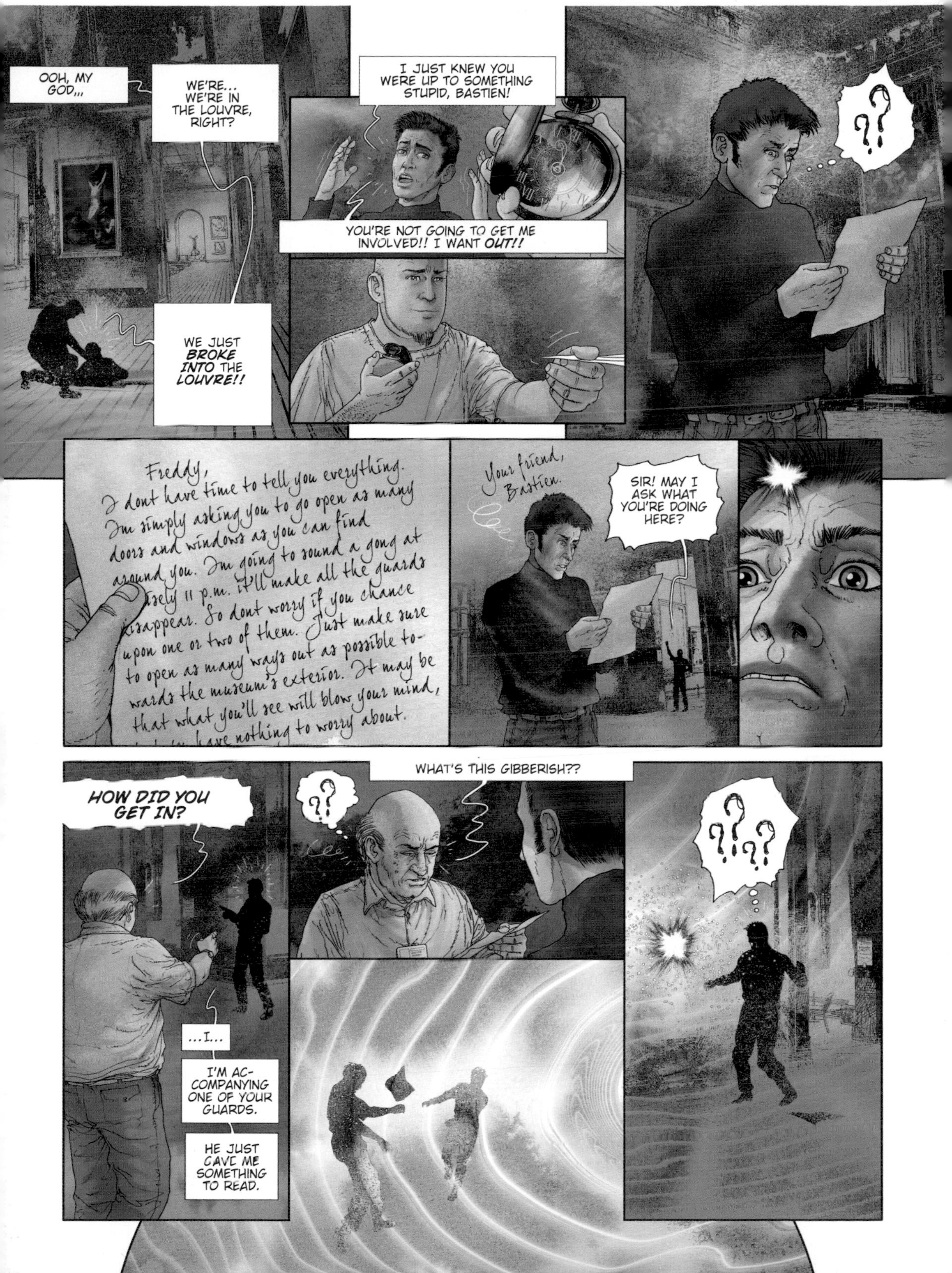
OOH, MY GOD,,,
WE'RE... WE'RE IN THE LOUVRE, RIGHT?
WE JUST **BROKE INTO** THE **LOUVRE!!**
I JUST KNEW YOU WERE UP TO SOMETHING STUPID, BASTIEN!
YOU'RE NOT GOING TO GET ME INVOLVED!! I WANT **OUT!!**
??
Freddy,
I dont have time to tell you everything.
I'm simply asking you to go open as many
doors and windows as you can find
around you. I'm going to sound a gong at
sely 11 p.m. it'll make all the guards
isappear. So dont worry if you chance
upon one or two of them. Just make sure
to open as many ways out as possible to-
wards the museum's exterior. It may be
that what you'll see will blow your mind,
have nothing to worry about.
Your friend, Bastien.
SIR! MAY I ASK WHAT YOU'RE DOING HERE?
HOW DID YOU GET IN?
...I...
I'M AC-COMPANYING ONE OF YOUR GUARDS.
HE JUST GAVE ME SOMETHING TO READ.
WHAT'S THIS GIBBERISH??
??
???

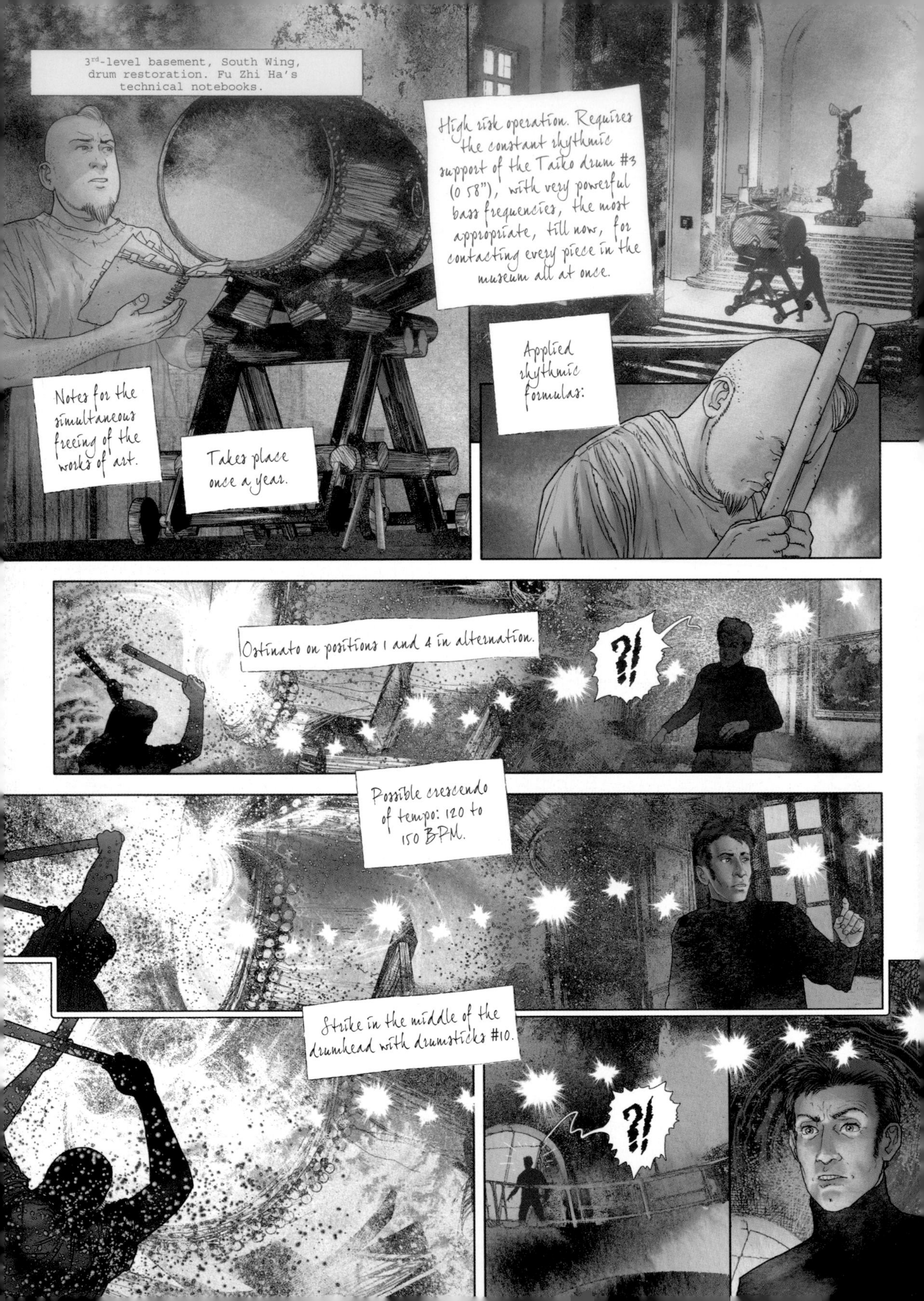
3rd-level basement, South Wing, drum restoration. Fu Zhi Ha's technical notebooks.
High risk operation. Requires the constant rhythmic support of the Taiko drum #3 (0 58"), with very powerful bass frequencies, the most appropriate, till now, for contacting every piece in the museum all at once.
Notes for the simultaneous freeing of the works of art.
Takes place once a year.
Applied rhythmic formulas:
Ostinato on positions 1 and 4 in alternation.
?!
Possible crescendo of tempo: 120 to 150 BPM.
Strike in the middle of the drumhead with drumsticks #10.
?!

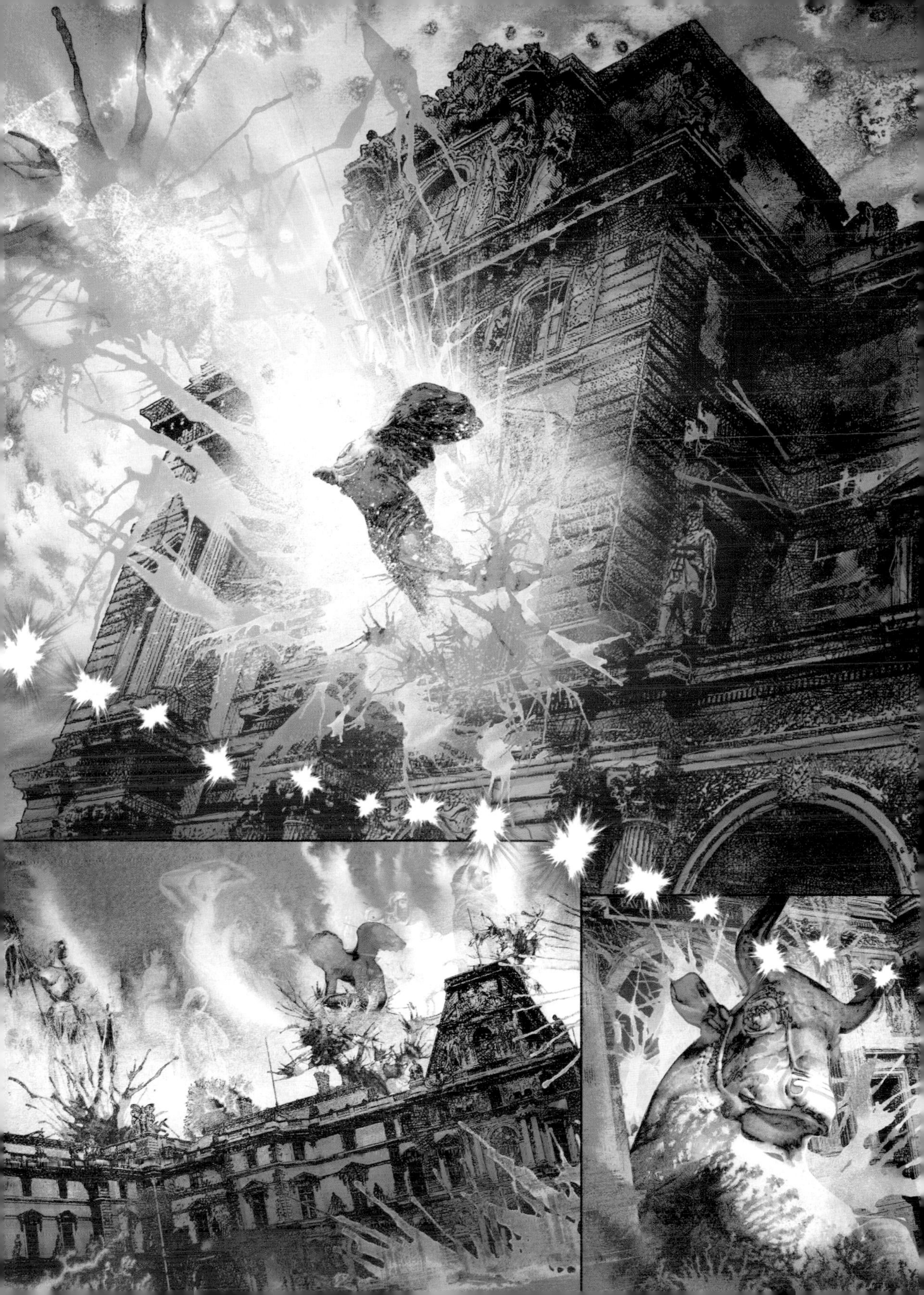

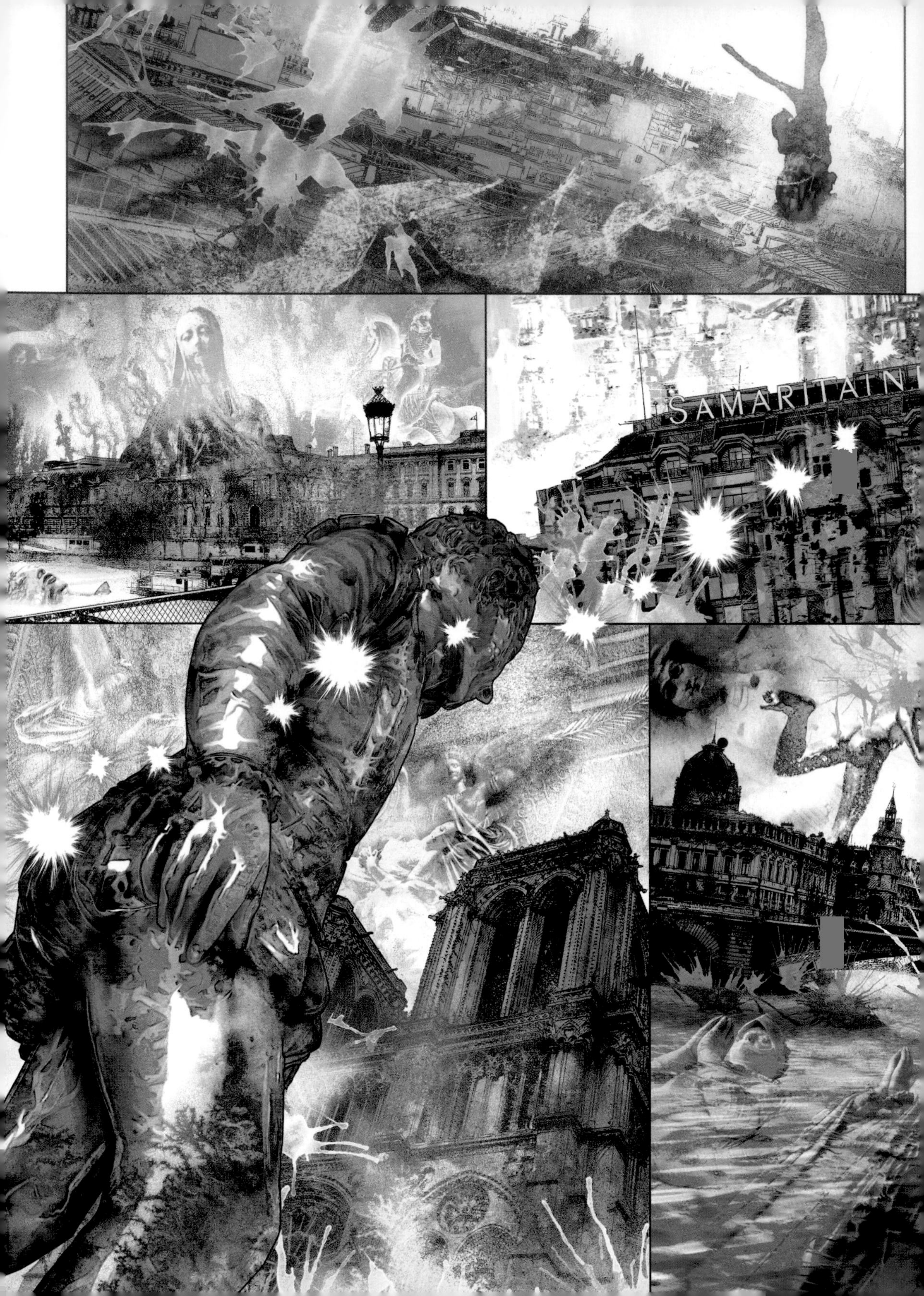
SAMARITAIN

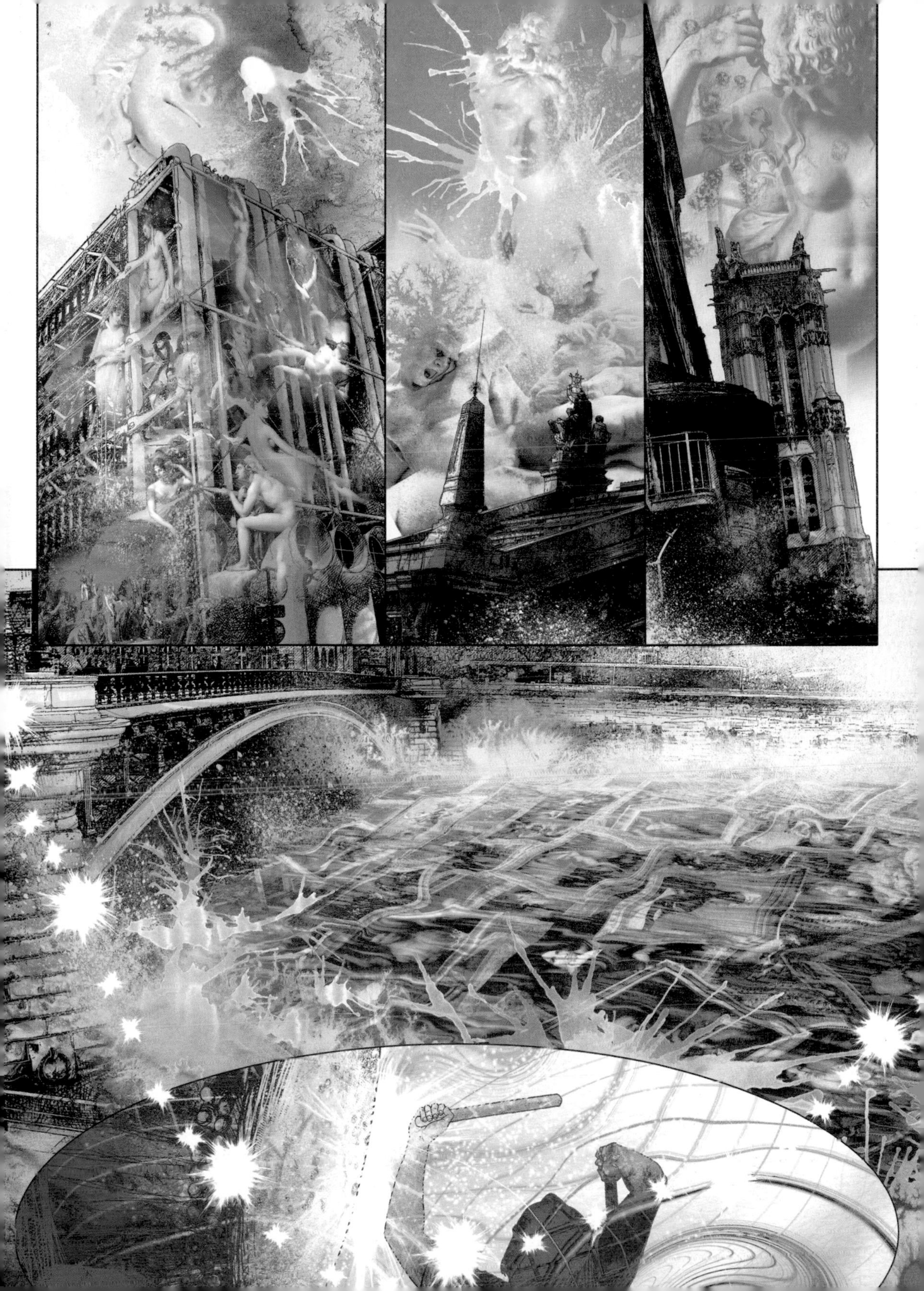

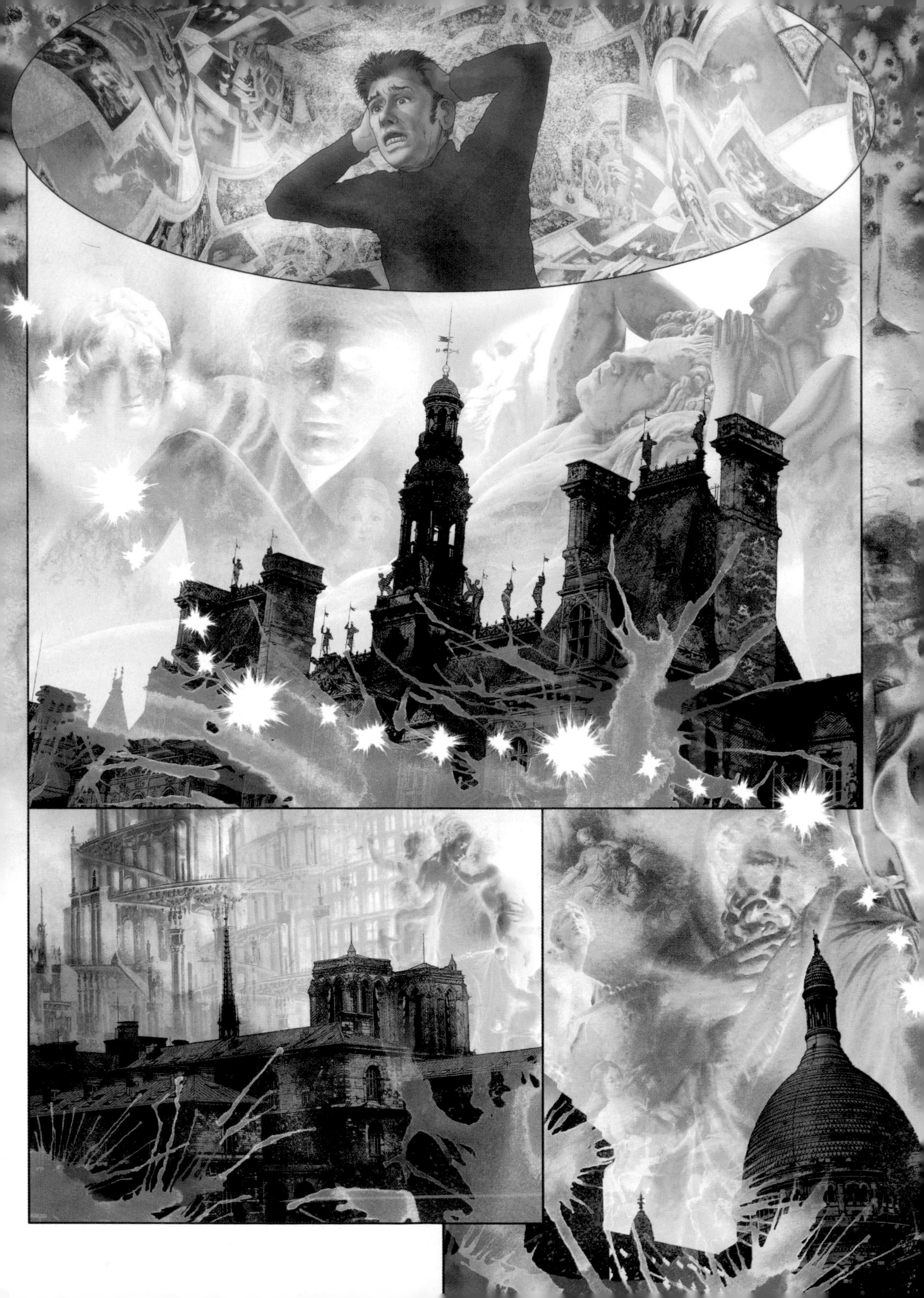

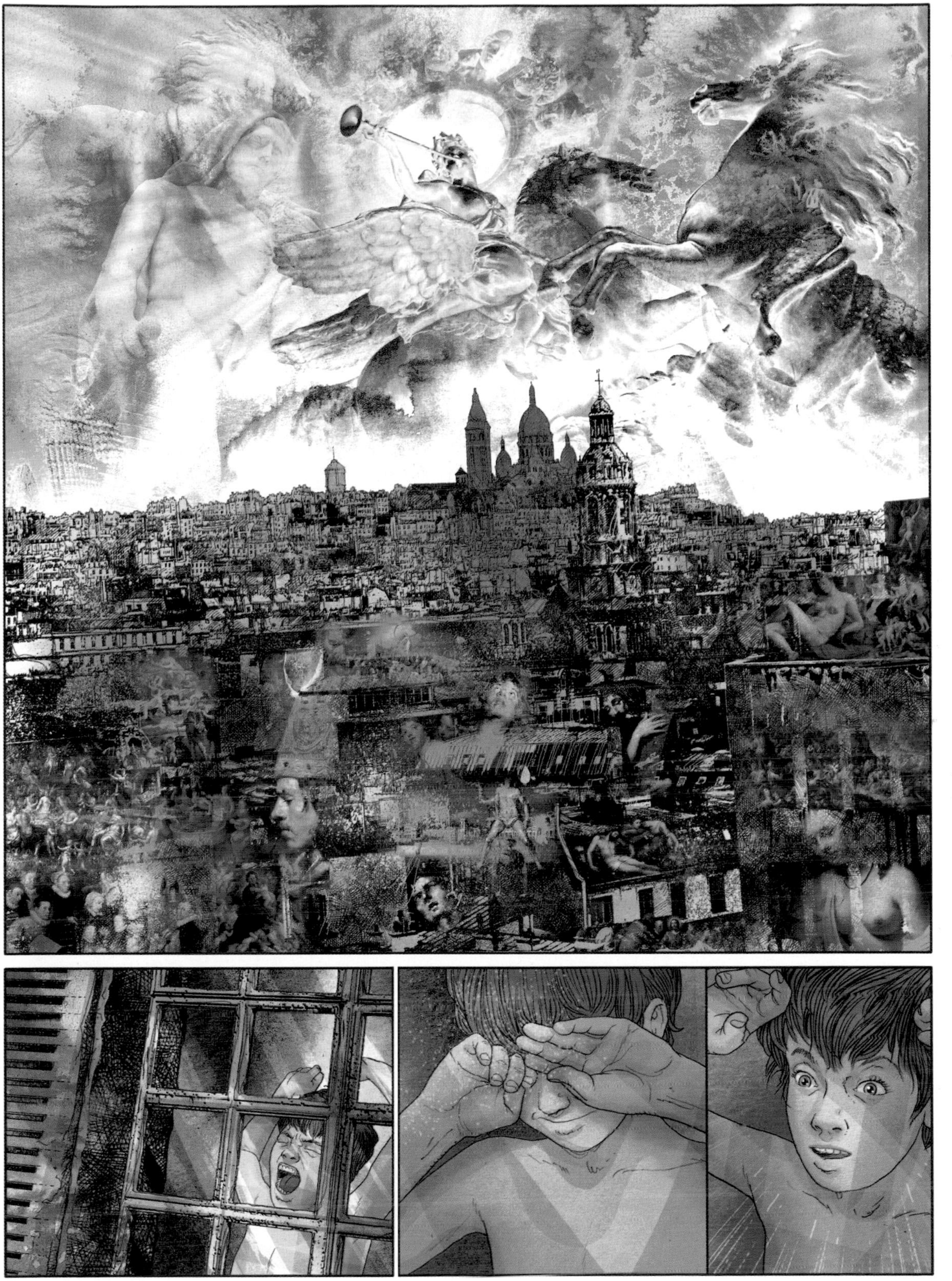

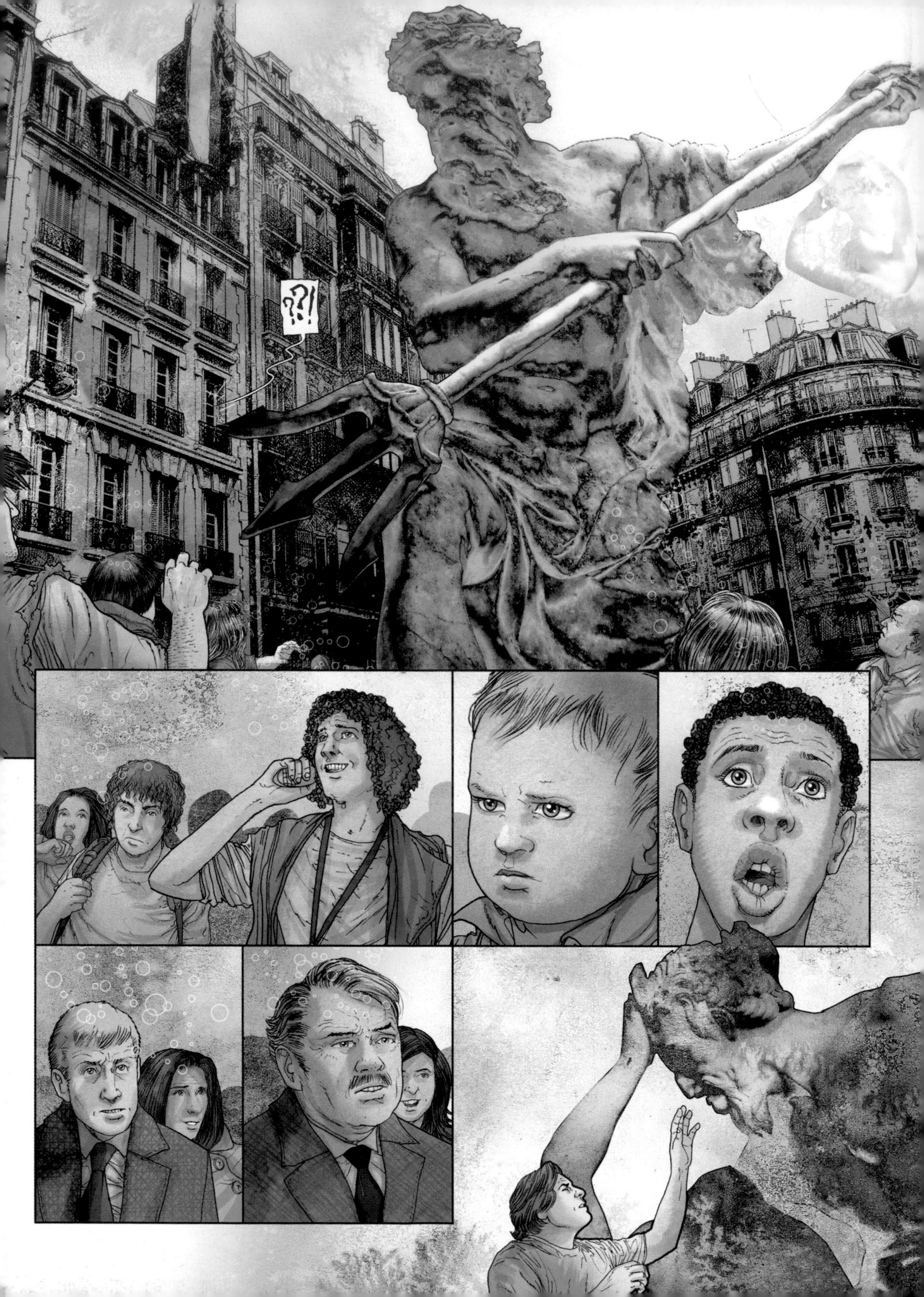

?!

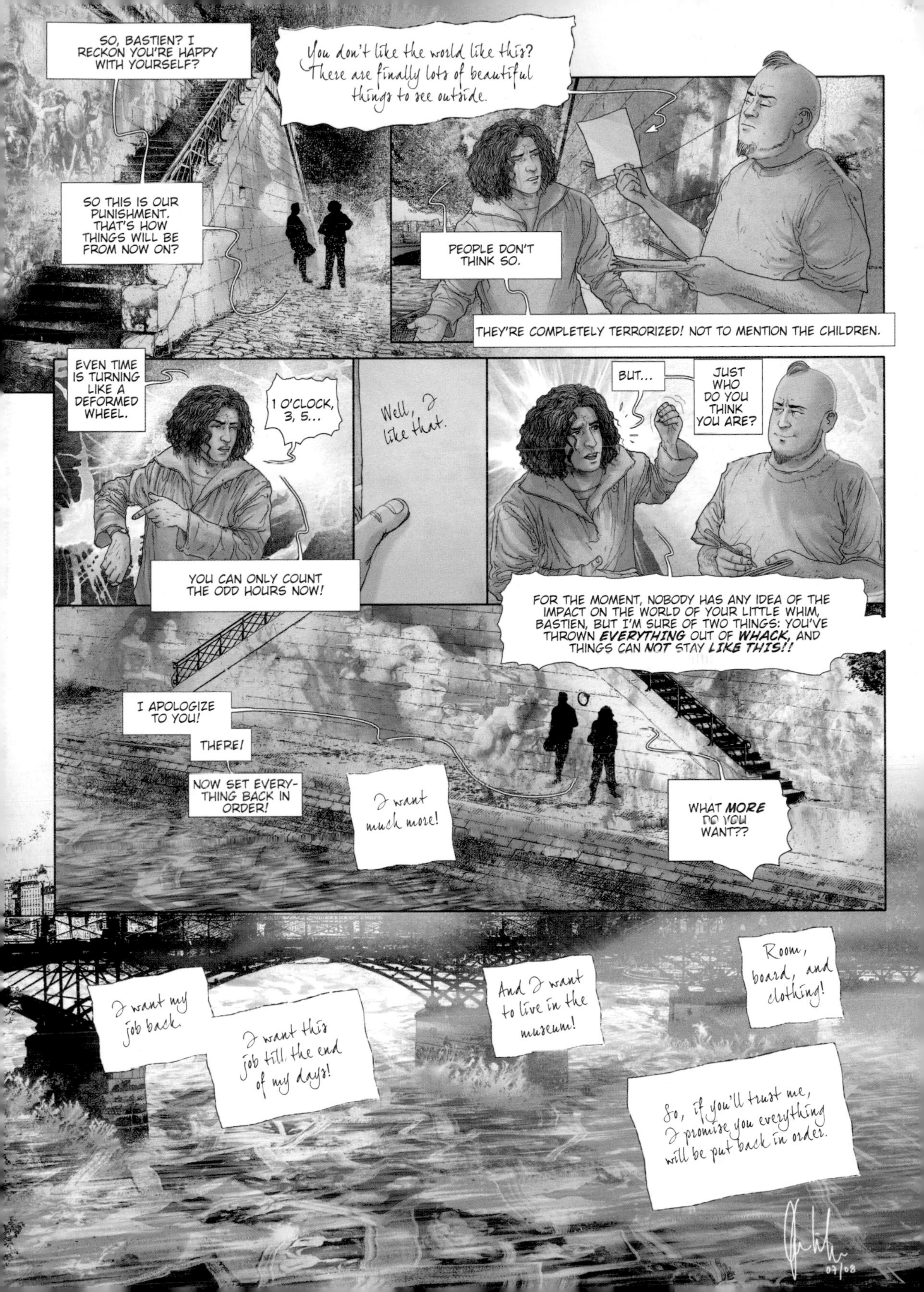

SO, BASTIEN? I RECKON YOU'RE HAPPY WITH YOURSELF?
You don't like the world like this? There are finally lots of beautiful things to see outside.
SO THIS IS OUR PUNISHMENT. THAT'S HOW THINGS WILL BE FROM NOW ON?
PEOPLE DON'T THINK SO.
THEY'RE COMPLETELY TERRORIZED! NOT TO MENTION THE CHILDREN.
EVEN TIME IS TURNING LIKE A DEFORMED WHEEL.
1 O'CLOCK, 3, 5...
YOU CAN ONLY COUNT THE ODD HOURS NOW!
Well, I like that.
BUT...
JUST WHO DO YOU THINK YOU ARE?
FOR THE MOMENT, NOBODY HAS ANY IDEA OF THE IMPACT ON THE WORLD OF YOUR LITTLE WHIM, BASTIEN, BUT I'M SURE OF TWO THINGS: YOU'VE THROWN EVERYTHING OUT OF WHACK, AND THINGS CAN NOT STAY LIKE THIS!!
I APOLOGIZE TO YOU!
THERE!
NOW SET EVERYTHING BACK IN ORDER!
I want much more!
WHAT MORE DO YOU WANT??
I want my job back.
I want this job till the end of my days!
And I want to live in the museum!
Room, board, and clothing!
So, if you'll trust me, I promise you everything will be put back in order.
07/08

A brief history of guardianship in the Musee Du Louvre
Report prepared with the kind assistance of Nathalie Trautmann

"In August 1796, the Musée du Louvre opens its doors to the public with some 600 works of art. The matter of their security is immediately called into question. For the moment, a request is made to the military, and thirty veterans will be assigned to this duty." [1]

Thanks to a portrait preserved in the Louvre and painted circa 1805 by David or one of his students, we are acquainted with the head of the thirteen first guards of the Musée Napoléon (the future Louvre), the Old Fuzelier. It is guessed that these thirteen first guards were grenadiers from Napoleon's armies, who, due to all-too meager military retirement benefits, had found themselves assigned to the Museum as guards in gratitude for services rendered and thereby to receive some financial benefit. "To display the works of art, to clean the rooms, and to see to security, there are barely thirteen then, after 1812, fifteen, working guards and two doormen. They all wear the uniform of the house of the First Consul, which, after 1805 obviously, becomes the richly brocaded livery of the Imperial house: a natural green dragoon outfit, a scarlet jacket, and braided hat. The robust doormen have all the flash of the Swiss Guards, with the braided cross belt, bearing sword and halberd." [2]

This sort of recruitment was later systematized in the 19th century. Up through 1982, the recruitment is done by mutual agreement, the positions are always reserved for veterans and, since 1976, to those entitled to benefits from the Commission for the Vocational Rehabilitation of the Handicapped. The first women join the ranks of this service in the Louvre in the 1970s.

In 1982, a competition is created in pursuance of the principle of equal access to public employment. A specific corps of guards in charge of the security of works of art and people thus was created: "agents for specialized surveillance in the national museums." In 1988, they become "agents for surveillance and conservation" under the aegis of the Ministry of Culture. In 1995, a

Fig. 1
Auguste Gérardin
The Apollo Gallery by Night,
circa 1880
Charcoal drawing with wash
Paris, Musée du Louvre
Department of Graphic Arts
© 2004 Musée du Louvre/Harry Bréjat

new status is inaugurated: "technical agents for reception, surveillance, and conservation." By way of these different designations, we can see the evolution of this profession, which is responding to the needs of a museum modernizing itself, as well as the lexical changes often betraying social concerns. In this respect, on January 20, 1793, year II of the Republic, mention is made of the primary task of a guard in the Louvre in a text signed by the minister of the Interior in which the former must "perform an inspection of the doormen and lamplighters of the Louvre, have the furnaces, stairs, and corridors swept, close the doors, receive and store the keys of vacant housing, alert the inspector of National Buildings of all known deterioration and repairs to be made [...], fulfill all the duties of the inspector concierge [...]." As of 1794, true guards would be recruited. Indeed, in that era, the word "guard" expressed a social advancement and was absolutely not perceived in a pejorative manner as it sometimes is nowadays.

1: Édouard Pommier, Reflections on the National Museum, monograph, Paris, 1992.
2: Dominique-Vivant Denon "Napoleon's Eye," exhibition cat., Paris, 1999, p. 132, chapter 5: "Dominique-Vivant Denon, First Director of the Louvre."

A few documents

Orders given by the Conservatory of the Central Museum of Art, for the military picket on guard, renewed daily at that post:

"Six of the seven guards of the Museum will make arrangements amongst themselves so that, every night, there will be one of them who sleeps in the gallery [...]. There will be supplied to the person on guard a bed which he will set up every evening and which will be folded up and locked away every morning; the cleaning of his bed linens will be taken into account; the Conservatoire will assume this expense." (June 30, 1795)

"The night guard will cry out during his rounds that pass the length of the garden upon the quay. He will not allow anyone, on the pretext of having his or her lodging facing on the garden, to be there after closing or before opening to the public [...]. Under no circumstance will he allow anyone to enter or leave the Museum by night via the garden; the sole exceptions are the museum doormen whose duty obliges them to make their night rounds [...]."
(July 25, 1795)

Record of Proceedings / Policy regulations for the employees of the Central Museum of Arts, decided upon by the Administrative Council during its session on the 25 Pluviôse Year V (February 13, 1797)

Article 7: " [...] The guards will wear attached to their buttonhole a silver plaque upon which are engraved the symbols of art and of surveillance. Its intent is to procure for the Museum guards the consideration that trustworthy employees deserve; fulfilling the expectations of the administration in this respect will depend upon their good conduct [...]." (fig. 2).

Article 11: "[...] Those who are guilty of the following infractions will be subject to the loss of their employment:
-any sort of proven untrustworthiness
-habitual drunkenness
-knowledge of an unreported theft [...]."

During the Third Republic (1870-1940) / Extract of the daily tasks of the guards, March 16, 1907, "Night shift"

"The guards, during the first years following their service entrance into the Louvre, are required to do night duty. This service is compensated by daily leave during daylight hours. They must perform rounds whose length is of about 3 miles, climb and descend 1400 stair steps, indicate their presence on 52 time clocks and sign their slates. After their rounds, they will stand guard and must clock in on every half-hour, under penalty of severe punishment."

Official Bulletin from the Ministry of War, Civilian and military positions reserved for the Army's enlisted and re-enlisted, Paris, 1911, "Guards of the National Museums," p. 100.

"In addition to the surveillance to be performed during the times when the public is admitted into the galleries, every day the guards of the National Museums must polish by foot the museum rooms, scrub the stairs, dust the paintings, climb a great number of stairs to supply heating, sawdust for the cleaning of the parquets, and, several times a month, make their night rounds. [...] The newly promoted guards must, for a period of two to three years, provide a special night service. Accordingly, they are on duty seven nights out of twelve, from 4 or 5 p.m. until 7 or 8 a.m. the next day, according to the season; but, otherwise, they have their entire day free to themselves."

1989 / Ordinance concerning the regulation of service for the personnel of the security corps of the National Museums; chapter two: night shift.

Article 36: "The principal missions of the security personnel on the night shift consist of taking preventive measures by putting into operation the alarm systems, of surveillance and intervention with respect to fires, theft or attempted theft, water damage, bomb threats [...]."
Article 39: "In addition to the direct surveillance of the collections, the surveillance personnel may be charged with special duties or be assigned to specialized services by the head of operations" (Notably, one of these services was to rewind the clocks spread throughout the museum).

Fig. 2

Silver plaque worn by the agents, then called "guards" of the Museum, 1796.

Paris, Musée du Louvre
Department of Objets d'Art.

© Musée du Louvre/Pierre Philibert

A Few Figures
Opening of the Museum:
13 military veterans
1811: 30 guards
1848: 37 guards
1874: 149 guards
1907: 166 guards
1915: 69 guards
1954: 64 guards
1993: 800 charged with
 reception and security
2008: around 1100 reception
and security associates

For us, the Deaf of France and of the world over,
the Musée du Louvre is well-known and much appreciated: first for
its famous collections of works of art, but also for its more recent
and no-less famous pyramid of glass. The lecture tours
in Sign Language, organized by lecturers themselves deaf,
of which the first took place in 1993,
are a huge part of this success.

The first deaf lecturers were trained at the Louvre,
one of the first places for bilingual education (French and French
Sign Language) in art history, sponsored by the International
Association of Visual Art for the Deaf, in conjunction with the Office of Museums
of France.

The Louvre wishes to share with the Deaf of all ages and all
nationalities, as individuals or groups, the richness and diversity
of its works of art (35,000 works in nearly nine miles of galleries).
The museum has set in place a policy of accessibility: lecture tours,
workshops, friday nocturnes, paired visits with a deaf
interpreter, and visio guides, all equipped with Sign Language.
Not to forget the audio-guides, equipped with magnetic loop antennas reserved
for the hard of hearing, and visitor leaflets written in different
foreign languages.

In 2002, the Musée du Louvre had the honor of receiving the certification of
"Tourism and Handicap" for its policy of accessibility towards the handicapped,
among whom the Deaf and Hard of Hearing, and continues to pursue its efforts.

Jennifer LIBERGE, deaf instructor
Jean-Paul PERBOST, national deaf lecturer

The making of this volume has been a unique experience.

My thanks to the Musée du Louvre for having been able to stroll about there on Tuesdays, with no public present, and to create that privileged contact with the works of art, which nourished the production of the project. To Fabrice Douar and his colleagues for their advice and their participation, Serge Leduc and the museum's night surveillance teams for having welcomed me into their ranks on the night of April 22, 2008, and Jean-Paul Perbost, a deaf lecturer.

My thanks to Sébastien Gnaedig and Futuropolis, for their consideration and trust.

Éric Liberge

Acknowledgments to the Musée du Louvre:

Henri Loyette, Didier Selles, Catherine Sueur,
Serge Leduc, Christophe Monin, Juliette Armand,
Soraya Karkache, Catherine Dupont, Moïna Lisowski,
Fanny Meurisse, Isabelle Calvi, Philippe Poncet,
Violaine Bouvet-Lanselle, Axelle Beth, Laurence Castany,
Adrien Goetz, Virginie Dumont, Yukiko Kamijima,
Masami Sakai, Nelly Girault, Élisabeth Laurent,
Chrystel Martin, Nathalie Brac de la Perrière,
Sabine de La Rochefoucauld, Robin Kopp, Zahia Chettab,
Marie-Cécile Bardoz, Guillaume Fonkenell,
Cyrille Gouyette, Nathalie Trautmann, Véronique Nollet.

To Carole de Vellou, Thierry Masbou, Patrice Régnier,
Cécile Bergon, Nathalie Trafford, Denis Curty, Christophe
Duteil, Pascal Cherry, Armande Bourgault, Cédric Béal,
Aline Sylla-Walbaum for their support.

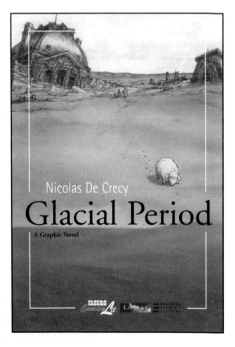

Nicolas De Crecy

Glacial Period

A Graphic Novel